The North

Edited By Machaela Gavaghan

First published in Great Britain in 2019 by:

Young Writers
Remus House
Coltsfoot Drive
Peterborough
PE2 9BF
Telephone: 01733 890066
Website: www.youngwriters.co.uk

All Rights Reserved
Book Design by Ashley Janson
© Copyright Contributors 2019
SB ISBN 978-1-78988-157-8
Printed and bound in the UK by BookPrintingUK
Website: www.bookprintinguk.com
YB0392L

FOREWORD

Here at Young Writers, we love to let imaginations run wild and creativity go crazy. Our aim is to encourage young people to get their creative juices flowing and put pen to paper. Each competition is tailored to the relevant age group, hopefully giving each pupil the inspiration and incentive to create their own piece of creative writing, whether it's a poem or a short story. By allowing them to see their own work in print, we know their confidence and love for the written word will grow.

For our latest competition Poetry Wonderland, we invited primary school pupils to create wild and wonderful poems on any topic they liked – the only limits were the limits of their imagination! Using poetry as their magic wand, these young poets have conjured up worlds, creatures and situations that will amaze and astound or scare and startle! Using a variety of poetic forms of their own choosing, they have allowed us to get a glimpse into their vivid imaginations. We hope you enjoy wandering through the wonders of this book as much as we have.

CONTENTS

Audley Junior School, Blackburn

Sanaa Ali (10)	1

Broadway Junior School, Sunderland

Blaine Sinclair (9)	2
Adam Bramley (9)	3

Clavering Primary School, Hartlepool

Amritha Maansi Pattar (7)	4
Amelia Alexandra Thompson (11)	6
Bella Canning (8)	8
Harry Wilson (7)	10
Erin Carr (7)	12
Emilia Gething (10)	14
Payton Everitt (7)	15
Leila Grace Matthews (9)	16
Martha Elizabeth Lakey (7)	17
Olivia Swinbourne (11)	18
Olivia Todd (10)	19
Farrah Wilkinson (9)	20
Theo Jaq Cooper (7)	21
Amelia May Elizabeth Nixon (10)	22
Cherri Tsang (10)	23
Imogen Elizabeth Burton (9)	24
Ariana Smith (10)	25
Amelia Steel (10)	26
Isaac William Kennedy (10)	27
Abbey Wood (10)	28
Lexi-Leigh Walton (10)	29
George Hender (10)	30
Ruby Beth Johnson (10)	31

Milly Rose Runham (9)	32
Lexi Gibson (9)	33

Embleton Vincent Edwards CE First School, Embleton

Caroline Brown	34
Mary Elizabeth Fentiman (8)	36
Tabitha Newman (10)	38
Max Butler	40
Jack Laurance Kelly (9)	42
Daniel Davison	44
Abbie Dodds	45
Josh Tavonesa (10)	46
Barnaby Mark Stanley Green	47
Alfie Jobling	48

Grappenhall Heys Community Primary School, Grappenhall Heys

Amalie Eve Potter (6)	49
Bebe Walkden (8)	50
Eva-Rose Faith Chong (6)	51
Amelie Hackett (6)	52
Poppy Richardson (8)	53
Serena Standring (8)	54
Aya Al-Rawi (7)	55
Orlaith Harris (6)	56
Finley Hackett (5)	57

Harrow Gate Primary School, Stockton-On-Tees

Vesper Leigh Urboda (9)	58
Robyn-May Howard (9)	59
Chloe Muir (10)	60
Jackson Mills (9)	61
Isaac Villacastel (9)	62
Preston Skipp (9)	63
Xyiana Jane Mendoza (9)	64
Matthew Go (9)	65
Teigan Jones (10)	66
A Ryder (9)	67
Jake Hunnam (9)	68
Grace Alice Robson (9)	69
Cory Screen (9)	70
Mason Lowery (9)	71
Lacey Conway (9)	72
Maddie Laura Sutheran (9)	73
Lexi Parkin (9)	74
Leon-Cole McQueen (10)	75
Olivia Grace Chantrell (10)	76
Layla May Travers (9)	77
Katie Leigh Mann (11)	78
Dameer Khan (9)	79
Leah Hackett (9)	80
Zac Edward Kightly (9)	81
Daisy Melissa Aberdeen (10)	82

Helsby Hillside Primary School, Helsby

Ava Williams (7)	83
Mary Eva Cottrell (8)	84
Amy Martindale (8)	87
Charis Catherine Bintliff (8)	88
Alistair Stead (11)	90
Blake Williams (10)	92
Neve Jones (7)	94
Grace Olivia Murphy (10)	95
Maisie Holding (7)	96
Reece Harley Donnelly (8)	97
Louie Nuttall (8)	98
Emily Davies (8)	99

Jake Antony Thakur (8)	100
Tiana-Nicole Grant (7)	101
Charlie Holding (9)	102
Imogen Marsden (8)	103
Daisy Buckthorpe (8)	104
Harry James Wilson (8)	105
Kaya Rose Howard (10)	106
Tilly Axford (7)	107
Lewis Stanley Plant (8)	108
Emma O'Hanlon (7)	109
Emily Lightfoot (7)	110
Sam Mozeley (10)	111
Conor Hayes (8)	112
Anabel Porter (10)	113
Heidi Edwards (8)	114
Noah George Morphet (7)	115
Mathieu Fell (7)	116
Heidi Fleming (7)	117
Amelia White (7)	118
Charlie Jackson (8)	119
Oscar Satur (10)	120
Cerys Rogers (10)	121
Ava Rose Pollard (9)	122
Nancy Farmer (10)	123
Louie Joseph Burns (9)	124
Bailey Sidney Kaye (7)	125
Lei Perry (10)	126
Oscar Walton (8)	127
Archie Coyne (7)	128
Paige Olivia Cowper (7)	129
Zoe Jade Littler (7)	130
Chiara Autumn Ferraro-Smith (7)	131
Brooke McBride (10)	132
Nooralhoda Al-Zubaidy (10)	133
Willow Walton (8)	134
Luca Mark-Aroon Singh (7)	135
Rose Slator (9)	136
Aleesa Pynadath (8)	137
Mia Skarnes (8)	138
Jacob Green (7)	139
Anthony Davidson (7)	140

Ladywood School & Outreach Service, Little Lever

Maisie Jayne Hall (10)	141
Casey Booth (10)	142
Thomas Edge (8)	143
Marcus Buckley (8)	144

Meanwood Community Nursery & Primary School, Rochdale

Vareen Hussain	145

Old Hall Primary School, Brandlesholme

Evie Morris (8)	146
Noah Budgen (8)	147
Daniel Taylor (9)	148
Charlie Collinge (8)	149
Ava Waterhouse (8)	150
Charlie O'Hara (9)	151
Brodie Keenan (8)	152
Jack Brooks (8)	153
Eva Smith (8)	154

St Aidan's RC Primary School, Ashington

Emily Turpin (8)	155
Lexi Hedley (8)	156
Jireh Eunice Lagmay (6)	157
Savannah White (8)	158
Evie Biswell (7)	159
Lewis Ligtley (7)	160
Emily Louise Richardson (7)	161
Narisara Fletcher (7)	162
Eva Scott (7)	163
Lily Williamson (7)	164
Mya Teasdale (7)	165
Nathan Catania (7)	166
Lilly Slater (7)	167
Lillani Grace McBride (7)	168
Franchesca Santos (7)	169
Jake Wheldon (7)	170

Harry Robson (8)	171
Charlie Mazzella (8)	172
Evie Grace French (6)	173
Jaden Tait (8)	174
Abbie Vout (7)	175
Olivia Hewitt (7)	176
Jack Robert Patrick Jarvis (8)	177

St Catherine's RC Primary School, Sandyford

Oliver Gracia-Ruiz (8)	178
Qasim Akhtar (8)	180
Amir Orand (8)	181
Chloe Logue (9)	182
Sarah Humphrey (8)	183
Grace Emily Dixon (9)	184
Mariya Z Wasif (8)	185
Neghot Abrehe (9)	186
Theo Robertson (8)	187
Anna Carr (8)	188
Nikki Garcia Kukilo (9)	189
Maisie Francis (8)	190
Matthew Morley (8)	191
Karen Shi (8)	192
Charlie Crass (8)	193

St Mary's Catholic Primary School, Crewe

Ewan Anthony Blud (9)	194
Theresa Cross (10)	195
Layla Finney (9)	196
Sophie Holly-Marie Cherrington (10)	197

The Firs School, Chester

Eline Streefkerk (9)	198
Frankie (8)	199
Thomas Bartley (8)	200
Seb Wilson (8)	201
Eliza Turner (8)	202
Zara Bickerstaff (8)	203

Temi Smith (8)	204
Lola May Bowden (8)	205
Josh Gratton (8)	206
Tia Lily Hughes (9)	207
Jack O'Keefe (8)	208
William Edward Mallon (8)	209
Abeer Vashisht (8)	210
Olly Jones (8)	211

The Willows Primary School, Woodhouse Park

Saanvi Nayak (10)	212
Mia McCaffery (10)	213
Lucie Hannah Oxley (7)	214
Summer Kirkham (7)	215
Hana Ahmed (9)	216
Dominique Palfreyman-Hawkes (8)	217
Chelsea Roscoe (10)	218
Ikshita Singla (9)	219
Alexis Grace Daniels (9)	220
Vincent Stringfellow (8)	221
Courtney Kavanagh (7)	222

The Poems

Long Hot Summer's Day

It was a long hot summer's day
Children came out to play
The sky was bright and blue
And it definitely wasn't a day to catch the flu
Children all happy and smiling
Whilst parents were inside ironing
Even though clouds were in the air
The sun would always be there.

Sanaa Ali (10)
Audley Junior School, Blackburn

Eight-Trunked Elephant

An eight-trunked elephant is a thing
It uses number two to help him sing

Trunk number three, all brown and starry,
Helps Ellie to find her way all night
Like a telescope or guiding light

Trunk four is to help him blow his nose

Eight-trunked elephant jumping up and down

Five to help him save his life
Seven to help him get ready
Eight to not be late for a date

One not to be judged.

Blaine Sinclair (9)
Broadway Junior School, Sunderland

The Cheeseburger Child Eater

An evil cheeseburger sits in its lettuce throne
Waiting impatiently for a nosy child
To try and make it their own
The child tries to munch with its big, greedy jaws
But the burger eats the child
And his friend for his main course.

Adam Bramley (9)
Broadway Junior School, Sunderland

The Sound Collector

Based on 'The Sound Collector' by Roger McGough

A stranger came this morning
Dressed all in black and grey
Put every sound into a bag
And carried them away...

The talking of the teachers
The creaking of the doors
The munching of the children
The sound of the aeroplanes
The dripping of the taps
The flushing of the toilets
The people using the hand dryers
The slamming of the doors
The jingling of music
While the children dance
The moaning of the teachers
In the staffroom
The swishing of the water
When I wash my hands
The shaking of the trees
All on the school grounds

The filing of the paper
The teachers stirring tea
The flickering when we look through books
The teachers typing on the computer.

A stranger came this morning
He didn't leave his name
He left us only in silence
Life will never be the same.

Amritha Maansi Pattar (7)
Clavering Primary School, Hartlepool

Outcast

The Rapids raced
Aki's heart pounded
Wolf's temple ached
But they carried on
They raced up the towering axe handle
They nestled on boulders ridden with moss
Aki struck a bright beast that bites
Embers spat at Wolf's nose

Wolf gazed upon Fast-Wet
Aki followed his gaze
"Where is the Fast-Wet Clan, pack brother?" barked Wolf
Aki didn't know how to answer
So he whined, "Long gone to the past."
The great bear had taken their three souls two summers ago
Aki spotted Torak
Aki was an outcast
And also hunted by Torak
Torak saw him
Wolf twitched

Aki grunted, "Run!"
Torak screamed, "The outcast is near!"
Indeed Torak, the outcast is near...

Amelia Alexandra Thompson (11)
Clavering Primary School, Hartlepool

The Sound Collector

Based on 'The Sound Collector' by Roger McGough

A stranger came this morning
Dressed all in black and grey
And put every sound into a bag
And carried them away...

The rustling of the trees
The ringing of the phone
The chatting of the teachers
The creaking of the doors
The munching of the children
The squeaking of the markers
The dripping of the taps
The closing of the cupboards
The thud of the feet in the playground
The cleaning of the cleaners
Until everywhere is clean
The scratching of the pencils
The rummaging of the books
The air of the hand dryer
The beeping of the photocopier.

A stranger came this morning
He didn't leave his name
He left us only in silence
Life will never be the same.

Bella Canning (8)
Clavering Primary School, Hartlepool

The Sound Collector

Based on 'The Sound Collector' by Roger McGough

A stranger came this morning
Dressed all in black and grey
And put every sound into a bag
And carried them away...

The rustling of the trees
The talking of the children
The dripping of the tap
The air of the fans
The shouting of Mr Stoddart
Telling us how to play
The sizzling sausages
Getting ready for people to eat
The hoovering of the cleaners
Making the carpets clean
The telling of the dinner ladies
Being very mean
The ticking of the clock
The screaming of Mr McAvoy
The squeaking of the chairs
The thinking of the children.

A stranger came this morning
He didn't leave his name
He left us only in silence
Life will never be the same.

Harry Wilson (7)
Clavering Primary School, Hartlepool

The Sound Collector

Based on 'The Sound Collector' by Roger McGough

A stranger came this morning
Dressed all in black and grey
And put every sound into a bag
And carried them away...

The talking of the children
The teaching of the teachers
The rustling of the trees
The blowing of the wind
The chatting of the parents
The ringing of the phones
The tapping of the pencils
The flapping of the paper
The munching of the children
Eating their packed lunches
The crackling of the eggs
In the dinner hall
The noise of the hand dryer
When it isn't turned off
The running of the children playing outside.

A stranger came this morning
He didn't leave his name
He left us only in silence
Life will never be the same.

Erin Carr (7)
Clavering Primary School, Hartlepool

The Pizza Sleepover

A couple of years ago
This story is true so
Stay on your couch
Be sure not to slouch
And I will unveil
This very funny tale...

I was having a sleepover with my friends
At this sleepover, we had made our own dens
We had just eaten our tea
It was pizza for my friends and me
And in my room, we walked in to see
The pizza slices were having a party!
Then with no luck at all
This is what made the party fall
We had just had pizza for our tea
"Oh no!" cried my friend and me
Then the pizzas whipped out their wands
Were they going to turn us into frog ponds?
"Avada Kedavra!" they cried.

Emilia Gething (10)
Clavering Primary School, Hartlepool

Surrounded By Noise

I am surrounded by noise...
Buzz! Buzz! Buzz!
A bee flying around my head
Bang! Bang! Bang!
My younger brother jumping on the floor
Squirt! Squirt! Squirt!
My dog sitting on the bottle of chilli sauce
Woof! Woof! Woof!
My dog barking
Moo! Moo! Moo!
A farmer's cow mooing
Beep! Beep! Beep!
A car is stuck in a traffic jam
Miaow! Miaow! Miaow!
The cat next door
Boogie! Boogie! Boogie!
There's a party over the road
Mum's about to explode
We are surrounded by noise
Just stop and listen!

Payton Everitt (7)
Clavering Primary School, Hartlepool

WWI Poppy Fields

Above my head
Down goes the setting sun
My last part of hope
In this horrific, desiccated land
Bang, bang the guns go
The shells fall into winter trenches, glum
With crumbs, lice and a lack of rum
Where the wind blows forever and always
Then out of the noise
Silence and peace explore the Earth
For one last time until...
Bang! There I go
Into a place where darkness rules Earth
Where the Devil roams
Where the caves and caverns echo
Then everything suddenly goes silent and freeze
The war is here now
World War One, 1914-1918.

Leila Grace Matthews (9)
Clavering Primary School, Hartlepool

In The Magic Box
Based on 'The Magic Box' by Kit Wright

I will put in the box...
A dog bouncing on a trampoline with a dress on
And a unicorn driving a car with a pig
And a TV show from the olden days.

I will put in the box...
A baby panda doing a photo shoot
Even colours from pencils
Also, a pony lying on a sunbed.

I will put in the box...
Fourteen Marthas dancing the tango
A shiny baby snake
And a magic, talking spellbook.

I will put in the box...
An emoji sleeping
A hundred children ruling the world
And a hundred children shouting.

Martha Elizabeth Lakey (7)
Clavering Primary School, Hartlepool

The Unicorn That Exploded

There was once a unicorn that was torn to shreds
It was pink and purple and only ate bread
One day, the unicorn was afraid
She woke up in an arcade
There were gumdrops everywhere
She couldn't handle the smell of them
Drifting through the air
She jumped around all the sweets
The drops were terrible treats
She fell forward and took a bite
This gave her a fright
Suddenly, she was in pieces on the floor
Some of them were rolling out the door
She could no longer eat her bread
She couldn't even be fed!

Olivia Swinbourne (11)
Clavering Primary School, Hartlepool

What Would It Be Like Down A Kitchen Sink?

My oh my, this is crazy to think
What it would be like down a kitchen sink
But would it be fun?
Maybe, if there's sun!
But how would I get back up?
The answer is in a cup
I could zoom up in the air
With the help of a grizzly bear
Or I could buy some wings
Perhaps from the five kings
Would it be dirty or would it be clean?
I don't know, maybe a dream
Perhaps I wouldn't like it down there
Maybe it would be a nightmare
I don't know where it would end
I might break and never mend!

Olivia Todd (10)
Clavering Primary School, Hartlepool

World War One

Down in Flanders Fields,
Jack and Gerald made it another night,
Christmas Day, they play football,
But as the bombs fall by boxing day,
They fight for another fortnight.
Allies and Central Powers battle away,
In the trenches, they hope and pray,
Tanks are used to clear the site.
Jack says to Gerald,
"RIP soldier good night."
Poppies lay as they cry,
And on a cold November night,
Germany fled that horror site,
Jack fell to his knees in sadness and delight.
1914-1918.

Farrah Wilkinson (9)
Clavering Primary School, Hartlepool

The Magic Box
Based on 'The Magic Box' by Kit Wright

I will put in the box...
Flying chocolate that flies upside down
And flies into my mouth
My wind-up tree that talks
And scares people all the time.

I will put in the box...
My horse that does backflips and front flips
My ball that talks and lights up in the dark
And my invisible bike that rides itself and talks.

I will put in the box...
Cats driving cars and snakes
And magic people flying.

I will put in the box...
Magic pencils that draw for you.

Theo Jaq Cooper (7)
Clavering Primary School, Hartlepool

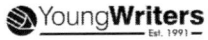

Birthday Party On Mars

Five, four, three, two, one!
Whoosh! Kaboosh!
Let's get the chocolate mousse
The party has started
The aliens have landed
A party hat they are handed

Mars bars are flying everywhere
Look, some are even in my hair!
I have eaten too many cupcakes filled with cream
Now my face is turning green!

The balloons are deflating
It's time to go home
But before I leave
My mum bought me a pet hamster
And I named it Leaf.

Amelia May Elizabeth Nixon (10)
Clavering Primary School, Hartlepool

Phantom

I entered the house
Without knowing what would happen,
Haltingly, I went in,
Ghostly lights surrounded me,
It felt like a spirit was haunting me!
I was trembling from head to toe,
Inside looked very eerie.

Every second I shuddered,
I'd seen a blood fountain
Flowing like a stream of red
With sounds of phantoms and ghouls.
All of a sudden, all those ghostly lights
And phantom sounds were gone...

Cherri Tsang (10)
Clavering Primary School, Hartlepool

World War 1

W andering soldiers, wandering bombs
O ver soldiers' heads, bullets fly
R un for your life
L earning to shoot the enemies' hearts
D emolishing friendships, demolishing lives

W orried soldiers, worried wives
A rmies invading territories
R ushing to dodge your death

1 914-1918.

RIP to all of the soldiers that died in WW1.

Imogen Elizabeth Burton (9)
Clavering Primary School, Hartlepool

The Abbey

Into the abbey I go,
I feel terror grow within.
The groaning floorboard tries to grab my ankle,
I desperately wish to be set free.

Dead bodies are all over,
Blood is dripping from the ceiling
Like someone is having a bloodbath.
I want to run back, but I don't know where to go,
It feels like devils are circling around me,
Red-eyed rats run all over...

Ariana Smith (10)
Clavering Primary School, Hartlepool

Sweet Land

I can see giant gummy bears
I can see a massive mushroom
I can see a chocolate waterfall

I can hear running on the grass
I can hear the jelly beans falling from trees
I can hear the chocolate smashing on the rocks

I can smell the mint drifting through the air
I can smell the air filled with chocolate
I can smell the sweet scent of strawberry gummies.

Amelia Steel (10)
Clavering Primary School, Hartlepool

A Walk In The Woods

As I walk in the woods,
A great shadow appears above.
I hear whispers ahead,
I then see a head
Poking up from a bush,
Waiting for me to come up close.

As I walk through the night,
I get a big fright.
I see an unusual sight,
It's standing in the moonlight.
As it stares into my soul,
It gets sucked into a black hole.

Isaac William Kennedy (10)
Clavering Primary School, Hartlepool

Chocolate Land

I can see giant gummy bears
I can see a huge mushroom dripping with caramel
I can see a chocolate river

I can smell sweet chocolate invading my nostrils
I can smell mint candy canes
I can smell fruity chewies growing on trees

I can hear peppermints dropping off the trees
I can hear chocolate running
I can hear jelly wobbling.

Abbey Wood (10)
Clavering Primary School, Hartlepool

Chocolate Land

I can see a chocolate waterfall
I can see colourful candy canes
I can see colourful jawbreakers

I can hear the chocolate waterfall splashing
I can hear candy canes breaking
I can hear slurping noises from the jelly

I can smell mouth-watering chocolate
I can smell giant strawberry gummy bears
I can smell everlasting bubblegum.

Lexi-Leigh Walton (10)
Clavering Primary School, Hartlepool

No Man's Land

Guns were fired rapidly at troops
No man's land was filled with barbed wire
Poppies grew where the men lay low
Soldiers received letters their wives

Machine guns were shooting at the Central Powers
Tanks got blown up by bomb dogs
Horses were carrying bags
Horrid battles happened in no man's land.

George Hender (10)
Clavering Primary School, Hartlepool

War Is Here!

In fields, poppies grow
Between crosses, row after row
Rats the same size as cats
Winds always blow
I don't want any more trench time
I simply want to go home
Banging, clanging and mustard gas
Explosions, emotions, broken sleep
War is here now
It is my turn to go...

Ruby Beth Johnson (10)
Clavering Primary School, Hartlepool

The Poppies

Some people were out there
When there was a war
People were shot to the floor
Everywhere the bodies lie
You can't hear a cry
The poppies grew in the snow
When the people surrendered.

Milly Rose Runham (9)
Clavering Primary School, Hartlepool

Haiku Poetry

A knock on the door
Fathers now in Flanders Fields
Families crying

War is over now
Lots of soldiers died for us
It was for freedom.

Lexi Gibson (9)
Clavering Primary School, Hartlepool

Rainbow Rider

When it rains, I sit outside
To wait and watch upon the skies.
My mother calls, "Come inside!
Oh Maisy, do come inside!"
But I'm just as happy here watching the rain go
Plip, plop, plip, plop on the pond.
"But Mother!" I call.
"I have to watch for rainbows in the sky, don't I?"
And no sooner than the words leave my mouth,
A rainbow springs in the sky
And, before my mother can tell me to
'Knock some common sense into my head',
I'm leaping up from the wet, green grass,
I'm leaping up into the sky
Like in storybooks when they fly!

Within moments, I'm high up above
In the fluffy, white clouds,
In the land of the Mystic Rainbows,
Which is where all the rainbows go when
The Weather Witch doesn't need them to show.
It's dark and bleak yet shiny and sleek,

It makes you smile,
It makes you glad,
It makes you happy,
It makes you sad,
And with all those emotions put into one,
It makes it one magical mystical time!

I'm soaring through the sky,
Looking for the rainbow I just saw,
Just then, I hear a voice: "Maisy, I'm over here!"
I fly to the voice and before I know it,
I'm on top of Rainbow Joyce!
Then sitting down upon her back,
I slide down and laugh with glee.
I slide down several times,
Then I hear my mother call me:
"Maisy, dinner's ready!"
So I say goodbye to Rainbow Joyce
And fly down to my garden,
And go inside for my tea,
But just before I go in, I whisper to myself,
"Goodbye Rainbow Joyce we'll meet again soon."

Caroline Brown
Embleton Vincent Edwards CE First School, Embleton

The Emergency Services

There's a penguin in trouble,
No need to worry,
Call 999 and they'll definitely hurry.
Here's paramedic Bunny,
Her sirens screeching loud,
Driving at full speed
As she pushes through the crowd.
Yes, here she is at last,
Penguin gasps that Bunny drives so fast.
Bunny pulls out a bandage
And wraps it round Penguin's arm,
Bunny relaxes Penguin by saying, "Keep calm."
Then she drives back to the hospital
To have a little rest,
"Now then," said Bunny, "put me to the test."

An elephant has stolen a bag of swag,
Oh no! They're playing hide-and-seek tag.
Police Puppy hides behind a bin,
What's that huge lump the colour of tin?
At last, Puppy catches him and puts him in a cage,
"Lock him in quickly!" now Elephant is in a rage.

The cars are roaring with ear-piercing sounds.
In that bag of swag there are trillions of pounds.
"Let's throw him into prison now, serves him right!
Go on, secure the lock very, very tight!"

It's a cold and wintery night
And the roads are filled with snow,
No problem for Kitten, she's on the go.
Her sirens are wailing, the lights are flashing,
The speed of the engine is terribly smashing.
There are scorching hot flames
Coming out of the flat,
The sounds of the engine are like a screaming cat.
Kitten pulls out a hose and starts to squirt,
"Don't worry everyone, I'm on alert!"
Now the fire is out at last.
"Wow!" someone said. "That was fast!"

Mary Elizabeth Fentiman (8)
Embleton Vincent Edwards CE First School, Embleton

Candy Land

I woke up in this strange land
And I could hear the sound of a band.
One of the members came over to me,
"You're in Candy Land but do not fret,
You just have to bet."
"Wait, what? Where am I?"
At that point, I thought they'd lied.
I looked around and saw
A melted gummy bear stream,
I acted like one big team.
Unmeltable ice cream trees,
Sadly, they had no leaves.
The floor was lollipops and liquorice
With melted marshmallows on top
And it didn't even flop!
Running around in the wildest way
Were gummy bunnies trying to play.
One hopped over and said,
"What time do you go to bed?"
"Eight o'clock," I replied, "why?"
"Because we're going to have cherry pie!"

I apologised and fake cried,
I said, "I can't, I have to go, I'm sorry!"
He said, "Do not worry."
He handed me a sweet treat,
"Lovely to meet-"
He ran away,
It was the only way.
His parents came over to me,
His mum said, "I'm a bumbling bee!"
They invited me back to their home
On top of an ice cream cone!
It looked like a castle, a gummy one,
Bouncing on it was so much fun!
It was rainbow-coloured and cute,
Unlike Dad's big boots,
It was like some sort of dream!

Tabitha Newman (10)
Embleton Vincent Edwards CE First School, Embleton

Monster Invasion

There I was, looking in the sky,
I saw something weird in the corner of my eye.
A small, green spacecraft
With something on the top,
It looked very weak, as if it might just drop.
I looked closely as it came down,
I saw some round creatures
With paws that were brown.
When the creature landed,
I could see that they were green,
In the air, they looked quite round
But they were as long as a bean.

I looked at them and they looked at me,
They went *boom, boom, crash*
As they smiled with glee.
The creature made so much noise
That it almost made me deaf,
I'm surprised nobody looked at them,
Not even the town chef.
The small, ugly monsters started to come over,

But suddenly, somebody came to me
In a Range Rover.

An ugly, round monster came out of the car,
It looked like the others but it had been kept afar.
The sun shone down on the four odd animals
Like a spotlight,
Four round monsters being shone by a light,
I knew for sure it wasn't right.
The hideous creatures seemed to walk away,
I hope I never see them again,
Especially not today!

Max Butler
Embleton Vincent Edwards CE First School, Embleton

Cat Danger

I took a train to London,
Where people were in pain.
Suddenly, I heard an evil noise!
Miaow! It was an evil cat,
I watched as he stole a hat.
He set houses on fire,
Attacked humans and called for reinforcements.
An army of cats came marching out of a house
And set London on fire!
But worst of all, they flew through Big Ben
And blew up Parliament.
The government escaped
And tried to shoot the cats
But the evil cats killed them.
There was a lot of police outside!
The evil cats agreed to attack the police
But got distracted by birds that screamed.
After that, the evil cats screamed and howled
And flew into Buckingham Palace
And attacked the servants.
The army ran after the evil cats

But there were lots of booms, bangs,
Miaows, thuds, and a crash.
Then the cats broke into the zoo
And shot the animals who flew.
Out into the blue sky, flying past with a sigh,
The cats said,
"If the zookeeper hadn't shot us with a cane,
There would be no pain!"

Jack Laurance Kelly (9)
Embleton Vincent Edwards CE First School, Embleton

The Cookie Fox

There the Cooke Fox lay,
Down in his dark cookie cave.
With nowhere to go, he stays in his home
With no one to help him comb.
Then the rain comes, the fox steps back,
Then the stones attack!
He hits the stones and takes a well-earned nap.

The cookie cave down, down under the ground,
The Cooke Fox is out, out into the wild,
He finds a city and runs there in a jiffy,
He tries to find a new home
But there isn't even a dome.

The stone people are there guarding a dome
With cookie people trapped inside a stone.
Whatever would the Cookie Fox do now?
He runs to the right to grab a thousand pounds.
"Want this money?" the fox says with a shout,
"Yes! Yes!" they plead with no doubt.
The fox opens the door with joy in his heart,
Only to see them eating jam tarts!

Daniel Davison
Embleton Vincent Edwards CE First School, Embleton

Night-Time Shift

People think extinct animals are gone for good,
But I know something they all should.
One night, when everyone was in bed,
The animals came back from being dead.
Myths became the truth
As unicorns took photos in a photo booth.
All the extinct and mythical animals met up,
As if the night wasn't crazy enough,
Cheese started to fall from the sky,
But I wouldn't eat it, it was all dry.
Then the sun started to rise
As people started to open their eyes.
But don't be scared, the animals didn't die,
They stopped eating cheese with a big, old sigh.
They ran to a place with many names,
But the most common was the Valley of Games.
Once they got there, they took a rest,
"Well done! You have passed the test."

Abbie Dodds
Embleton Vincent Edwards CE First School, Embleton

The Flying Burger

The flying burger flies in the air,
Next to the seagulls and crows,
It runs on ketchup and mustard,
When it lands, the wheels start to screech.
When you get started, you just take a bite.
When the burger was on the road, someone came
And started coming towards the giant burger.
They pulled out their phones and *click, click, click!*
As fast as a lizard, the flying burger took off,
Up and up it flies.
Looking down from the burger,
You can see the light and the sky.
It's winter now, it's all frosty
And the burger is snowy and icy.
On the road, the burger drives
With a big bite from a fight.
At night, someone snuck in
And ate it when it was asleep!

Josh Tavonesa (10)
Embleton Vincent Edwards CE First School, Embleton

Veg Busters

One day, when a kid had broccoli,
He shrieked with a piercing squeal
Because there was veg on his plate,
He wouldn't eat his meal.

So he called the Veg Busters' name
Boom! those superheroes came.
The Veg Busters weren't very tall.
They couldn't reach the window
So they exploded through the wall

The Veg Busters busted in
And put the veg in the bin.
After that, the boy ate his meal
And no longer did he squeal.

But the joke was on his mum and dad
As the price for the new wall was mad.
So children, never fear
As the Veg Busters are always near!

Barnaby Mark Stanley Green
Embleton Vincent Edwards CE First School, Embleton

A Panda Race

There's a panda race in the bamboo forest hills,
Six pandas racing all throughout the day.
The race begins and already,
A panda bangs into a bamboo tree!
A bunch of leaves come off.
The panda sleeps in its sphere,
It hears a bee ready to sting its bum!
The panda bounces up and down
Into a pond full of fish, *splash!*
All the other pandas go *bang* and *boom!*
Two left, one wins,
In the end, the pandas say, "Good race!"
And they all get their medals.

Alfie Jobling
Embleton Vincent Edwards CE First School, Embleton

Time Travel To Candy

A time-travel machine sparkled
When two girls came to see.
As soon as they got in,
They found a big surprise.
They found lots of buttons
And pressed one five times.
Boom! They zoomed away
Into a new world for a whole day.
They crashed into lollipops
And before they could even breathe,
One said, "Wow, this is too cool, even for me!"
They ate lots of candy until they wanted no more
Then they decided they wanted to go home
"Bye!" they said and off they went home,
But when they got there,
There was candy in their beds!
Then they went off to sleep.

Amalie Eve Potter (6)
Grappenhall Heys Community Primary School, Grappenhall Heys

A Cheese's School Day

The teacher came in early
Our teacher is called Mr Stilton
He really was the smelliest teacher
Behind him, the flowers were wilting

The parmesan was a hard bully
The cheddar was very wise
The mozzarella was really focused
And the Edam told porky pies

We went on a school trip to the zoo
We were all scared of the alligrater!
The food it was eating was disgusting
I wish I'd eaten my lunch much later

We were absolutely exhausted
But after school, we had kung fu
We were all extremely boiling
"Argh! We've melted into fondue!"

Bebe Walkden (8)
Grappenhall Heys Community Primary School, Grappenhall Heys

Candy Land

Sophie strolled around the land
She met the candy king
Always making candy, even while he sings!

They fell in love
Sophie became the candy queen
She plopped into the river,
Because she was so keen!

She was sinking deeper and deeper
Until she heard a chirpy voice say,
"Grab my wing!"
It was the candy bird

She gripped his wing and took a ride
Way up to the sun
He flew her home
"Goodbye," she said, "my candy time is done."

Eva-Rose Faith Chong (6)
Grappenhall Heys Community Primary School, Grappenhall Heys

Bella And The Magical World

Bella sat down on a beautiful day
Her picnic was huge, she felt so lucky
She was about to take a bite of a cookie
When it said, "Please don't eat me!"
On a sticky, cheesy web
Was a burger on his chip legs
And he said, "Yes, don't eat us!"
But a star-shaped lollipop
Had a label that said: 'Lick me!'
One lick and she was away to a magical world...

Amelie Hackett (6)
Grappenhall Heys Community Primary School, Grappenhall Heys

What Am I?

I am a monkey that is very funky
I am funny but I don't have money
I will smash you up with a crash
I am silly but my name is not Billy
I live in the mountains
I like chocolate fountains
I eat bamboo
I don't shampoo
I am black
I will attack
I may be small but I can fight for the China wall.
What am I?

Answer: A gorilla.

Poppy Richardson (8)
Grappenhall Heys Community Primary School, Grappenhall Heys

Giant Play

One day, I met a giant
And played hopscotch with him.
He turned me into a giant too,
He said his name was Jim.
We jumped from one to ten
And I said, "I want to be a little girl again!"
So Giant Jim shrunk me in a whirl
Back to being a girl!

Serena Standring (8)
Grappenhall Heys Community Primary School, Grappenhall Heys

The Space Cookie!

Space cookie flying high
Soaring past comets nearby
Sparkle, pop, fizz, whizz!
Let's start the space quiz
Dip, dunk, crunch, munch
Try to guess what it is...

Aya Al-Rawi (7)
Grappenhall Heys Community Primary School, Grappenhall Heys

Love

Love looks like pretty birds flying high
Love feels like warm cuddles
Love sounds like chocolate crunching in my ear
Love tastes like hot chocolate
Love smells like flowers.

Orlaith Harris (6)
Grappenhall Heys Community Primary School, Grappenhall Heys

London Buses

London is so big
See the city on a bus tour
A red bus
A blue bus
Or even on a duck bus!

Finley Hackett (5)
Grappenhall Heys Community Primary School, Grappenhall Heys

A Haunted Night

In the middle of the night
The moon was shining super bright
I crept out of the door
And onto the dark moor
I packed myself a torch and some garlic or two
And went into the haunted house
With my black cat too!
As I crept into the house
A silhouette caught my attention
It was the ferocious Dracula, the ruler of the night!
I ran out of the house
But I woke up in my bed...
"Phew, it was a dream!" I said...

Dracula got out of his coffin
And stared at the moon
"It's past noon," he muttered
"I'll have to go hunting soon."
He got dressed in his famous attire
Then put on his cloak
He did his hair and gave it a little poke
As he wondered, "Should I have cow or human?"

Vesper Leigh Urboda (9)
Harrow Gate Primary School, Stockton-On-Tees

Are Ghosts Real?

You wake up but it's night
The lights are slowly flickering
You get the biggest fright of your life
Then you see a shadow flying at max height
You wonder with no delight
Are ghosts real?
Then you turn around
But the shadow is gone
You think you might die
You jump back into bed
And sleep for the rest of the night.

You wake up, it's not night
You have no fright
The lights have stopped flickering
You have delight in what you see
And there's nothing above you
You're not going to die
You ask your mum, "Are ghosts real?"
She doesn't respond
But what a night you had!

Robyn-May Howard (9)
Harrow Gate Primary School, Stockton-On-Tees

My Pet Rock

I own a pet rock who wears a croc
We go on walks but sometimes he squawks
He doesn't bite but he likes to fly kites
When Rock sees a clock
He turns around and does the pop lock
My pet rock is a lump
But sometimes he sneaks out a little pump
Bouncing all around, side to side
And up and down
Rock can run a mile and sleep for a while
He likes to eat gold
Thank God he isn't old!
My pet rock likes reading books
Also, he is a very good cook
Me and my pet rock have been
Through some rocky times
I've just realised how much this poem rhymes!
My pet rock is my best friend
We will be together until the end.

Chloe Muir (10)
Harrow Gate Primary School, Stockton-On-Tees

Mythical Creatures

Dragons flying through the sky
Dragons that are so high
Their wings are far
Aliens fly through the stars
And shoot their beams
Aliens are more powerful than they seem
Zombies come into the scene
And through the screen
Zombies come back from the dead
To eat the brains from your head
Dragons climb up to my bed
Dragons are above my desk
Dragons roar under the floor
Then aliens from outer space knock on my door
They know where to go and they crash
The zombies are there to break my chair
Zombies can't bear daylight
Dragons shine and fly light
Dragons like the dark night
And fly to a certain height.

Jackson Mills (9)
Harrow Gate Primary School, Stockton-On-Tees

House Of Fright

You will need a lot of might
To enter the House of Fright!
Yes I mean it when I say the House of Fright
Trust me, there will be a lot of monster bites!

Be aware of decapitated heads
And worst of all, people back from the dead
Don't cut your neck on the sharp thread
Otherwise, you really will be dead.

Don't hurry to evacuate
After all, this is a cage
Oh come on, be a mate
Hmmm, just try to escape.

You probably think there's a map
Oh come on, didn't you know it was a trap?
If you really want to be a champ
Try to escape this trap...

Isaac Villacastel (9)
Harrow Gate Primary School, Stockton-On-Tees

Burger Town

I found a rocket that crashed into the floor,
It was unusual, I had never seen it before.
I was confused but I knew it could fly
So I got in the ship and began to fly!
A planet was seen, shaped like a bun,
I peered at it, it looked like fun!
I travelled there, I was almost there,
Then I had a stare, then a glare.
I finally made it,
I stood on the thing and heard something,
It was like a zing,
It was Burger Town!
I took a chew, or maybe a few,
I am still here to this day,
If you want, you can come and stay!

Preston Skipp (9)
Harrow Gate Primary School, Stockton-On-Tees

Darkest Wood

In the dark night
You have no sight
Try not to get lost
Or you will be in a fright.

When the sun goes away
Monsters come out to play
Be careful of what you hear and see
Or else the monsters will catch you and me.

All the children try to run away
But little do they know, they can't escape
The children don't know what to do
However, the monsters are preparing
To make children stew!

In the dark night
You have no sight
Try not to get lost
Or you will be in a fright...

Xyiana Jane Mendoza (9)
Harrow Gate Primary School, Stockton-On-Tees

Water Vapour

Crashes, bashes, the ocean dashes
The sun is boiling, the water is thrashing
Invisible water is in the air
Use a microscope, if you dare
The fish and sharks have a dream
To be bouncing on the clouds, being free
If it's true, the water vapour will sprout
In the sky and in one week's time
It's a cloud and it's proud
As it flows through the sky
It goes to its friends, flying high
Then the cycle starts again
Crashing, bashing, the ocean's dashing
The sun is boiling, the water thrashes.

Matthew Go (9)
Harrow Gate Primary School, Stockton-On-Tees

My Food Friends

When I get home,
I am not alone.
With all the food,
I am not in a mood.
I call, "I'm home!"
Then the magic begins...

Everyone comes out
And walks about.
They come and find me,
But don't let me be!

We have lots of fun,
We even go and run.
We go around the house and the rooms
Before my parents get home.

They get home
So I'm not alone
I shout, "Quick, get back in place!"
Nobody is misplaced
My foods are my friends!

Teigan Jones (10)
Harrow Gate Primary School, Stockton-On-Tees

Aliens In Space

Aliens in the air
Playing very fair
The UFO on the moon
In the space gloom
There was a boom
The alien has a baboon
A space butterfly is in a cocoon
Now passing by is a space butterfly
How many eyes can you see?
One, two, three, four, five!
The baby is called Clive
He has five eyes
The baby cries for a million miles
He could fill the sea and isles!
He has two feet
His dad has four
And on each foot, they have four toes
His mother has fifteen feet with seventy-two toes!

A Ryder (9)
Harrow Gate Primary School, Stockton-On-Tees

Football World

Where is the ball?
Who is the best of all?
Who is the captain of the team?
The steam is coming through the machines!
They cheer on the team, "Go on!"
The keeper saves a rocket shot
His palms grow red and tingle a lot
Half-time strikes just in time
Off the players go in a line
Oranges the players eat
Aches and pains from their heads to their feet
Last gulp of water down the hatch
Out again to win a match
At eighty-nine minutes, they score
To the top of the league they go!

Jake Hunnam (9)
Harrow Gate Primary School, Stockton-On-Tees

The Prince And Princess

In a little castle
They had a little hassle
Over which prince to choose
As soon as they chose
Their prince rose
And they set off to their own castle
They felt amazed
Then they heard the gate
They went into it
The prince and princess sat down
With their golden crowns
And they could hear a tingling sound
Their food was ready
They walked steadily
After their feast
The king saw a beast
In a flash, the knight darted out
He slew the beast
And had another feast.

Grace Alice Robson (9)
Harrow Gate Primary School, Stockton-On-Tees

Dogs

Dogs in the night can be a fright
Although they are cute, they can bite
Bones and toys are their delight
In a furry basket, they sleep at night
Because they are small, they can hardly be seen
They eat, eat and eat
In my sight, there is no light
We have dogs
One of them is called Mia
One of them is called Charlie
And one of them is called Bobby
One of them is small
One of them is big
And finally, the last one is an unusual size!

Cory Screen (9)
Harrow Gate Primary School, Stockton-On-Tees

Crazy Creatures

In their little home
As big as they have grown
They are feisty and they are mighty
They love a little fight
One has supreme eyes
One has cream eyes
One is called Mary
One is called Scary
Two have two toes
Three have three toes
Some have little eyes
Some have big eyes
And some may have more!
They have crazy doors
They have fuzzy doors
They have big doors
They have small doors
And many more are to come!

Mason Lowery (9)
Harrow Gate Primary School, Stockton-On-Tees

Fantasy World

Stamp, stamp, don't be in a fright
Stamp, stamp, in the night
Stamp, stamp, the elephant's noise
Stamp, stamp, there's a lot of boys
Yum, yum, the cookies can stay
Yum, yum, the food, then we play
Yum, yum, the nuggets fry
Splash, splash, goes a mermaid's tail
Stamp, yum, splash! Everyone weeps
Stamp, yum, splash! Everyone sleeps.

Lacey Conway (9)
Harrow Gate Primary School, Stockton-On-Tees

My Nurse Is A... Unicorn

My nurse is a unicorn
I like her medicine the best
It tastes like elderflowers
When I'm feeling down
It's like she has a magic power
When I turn around
She's always there to see me
She must be busy
She's always there as a play nurse/unicorn
Outside it is never raining
Because when Miss Sparkle is near
She always makes the sky,
And everywhere, a better place.

Maddie Laura Sutheran (9)
Harrow Gate Primary School, Stockton-On-Tees

A Magical Unicorn

A magical unicorn sparkling in the night's sky,
You look so beautiful in the secret wonderland
And as you go through the magical forest,
There will be lots of rainbows
And beautiful waterfalls.
Fly through the air with your magical wings
And show off your magical horn.
Let your rainbow hair flow through the wind,
Your majestic tail will catch
All of the other animals being magical.

Lexi Parkin (9)
Harrow Gate Primary School, Stockton-On-Tees

Trippy Night

A fright and the monsters bite
Come in the night
The zombies come with all their might
The clowns don't know what is right
Graves lie with bodies in sight
Blood is scattered with delight
Try not to be terrified
When you are crucified
Before the day comes to enlighten you
High in the sky, the moon lies
And shimmers upon the creepy sight.

Leon-Cole McQueen (10)
Harrow Gate Primary School, Stockton-On-Tees

A Sleeping Unicorn

Ssh, ssh, up and down,
Ssh, ssh, there's a crown,
Ssh, ssh, there's a door,
Ssh, ssh, give me more,
Ssh, ssh, there's some corn,
Ssh, ssh, there's a sleeping unicorn,
Ssh, ssh, let's give her corn,
If you see the yellow unicorn,
You would think that she was just born
But be aware, she's lying next to thorns...

Olivia Grace Chantrell (10)
Harrow Gate Primary School, Stockton-On-Tees

Unicorns And Candyfloss

Unicorns are pretty
Candyfloss is tasty
The unicorns fly to space
The candyfloss has a taste
Of blueberry, cherry and raspberry too
Mmm, so yummy!
The edible pencils are the best
Now the unicorn needs a rest
He takes his candyfloss-flavoured toothpaste
And brushes his teeth in satisfaction
And then he goes off to bed.

Layla May Travers (9)
Harrow Gate Primary School, Stockton-On-Tees

Raining Cheese

Cheese, cheese, cheese
Sometimes it might land on trees!
You put it on food
And it changes your mood.

It's made out of milk
It feels like my favourite fabric, silk
Maybe animals eat it
But only a little bit!

Raining cheese coming from the sky
And everyone wondering why...

Katie Leigh Mann (11)
Harrow Gate Primary School, Stockton-On-Tees

There Was A Toilet That Never Flushed

The toilet that never flushed
I found it in a bush
All the leaves were pouring down
So I had a big frown
I made it float in a boat
Whenever I flushed it
The water came up
So I got a cup that got stuck inside
And went *ding!*
Then it went *fling* with a *ding, ding!*

Dameer Khan (9)
Harrow Gate Primary School, Stockton-On-Tees

Animals Of The World

Wow, what a sight!
Wow, mountain gorillas, what a fright!
Crack, crack, the gorillas break boulders
Crack, crack, the gorillas get rough
Stomp, stomp, the rhinos march
Stomp, stomp, the rhinos run.

Leah Hackett (9)
Harrow Gate Primary School, Stockton-On-Tees

Unusual Friends

Go into the deep sea
And find a squishy entity.
Be wary when you go to greet,
Shocked you will be from his feet.
He will keep predators at bay
So with my friend, I will stay,
"Jellyfish, please lead the way!"

Zac Edward Kightly (9)
Harrow Gate Primary School, Stockton-On-Tees

My Pet Fly

I have a pet fly
It shoots up into the sky
Sometimes it eats my crisps
Then I punch it with my fists
Sometimes I wish it would die
And if I were you
I wouldn't get a pet fly!

Daisy Melissa Aberdeen (10)
Harrow Gate Primary School, Stockton-On-Tees

My Adventure With Petal

I have a pet dragon called Petal,
Her scales are hard and shiny like metal.
I jump on her back and we fly through the sky
As I see other dragons passing by.
We land in a field of golden corn
And I see a horse with a horn.
We keep on flying until we land on a mountain
And Petal sees a yeti shouting.
Me and Petal have a little rest
Before flying back to her nest.
We meet a fairy who thinks Petal is scary
But I say, "Don't be wary!"
We have a picnic on a bench
And jam sandwiches and juice
And then I see a moose!
Me and Petal play in a band
And we play the flute with a music stand.
It has come, the time to fly back to Petal's nest
And have another rest.
We have had a busy day
And it is the end of our playtime day.

Ava Williams (7)
Helsby Hillside Primary School, Helsby

My Wonderful Walk To School

On my way to school today,
I got a huge surprise,
I skipped up the pathway
And could not believe my eyes!
Sitting right outside the shop,
All furry, blue and rude,
Was a monster with long, chicken legs,
Eating fishy food.
I watched him pick his gooey nose,
Then turn to me and growl,
"What you looking at nosy pants?"
With a moody, sulky scowl.
I tugged Mum's hand and
Pointed out the monster skulking there,
"It's just a teenage boy," she said,
"And it's very rude to stare."

As we walked towards the nursery,
Grazing on the grass,
I saw a candyfloss-pink unicorn

With a bottom full of gas.
He parped and pumped and boffed
And trumped with such a rippling blast,
Then tossed his silver, silky mane
And neighed as we went past,
"Those cauliflowers and spinach leaves
Were really rather yummy,
but eating them for breakfast was
A nightmare for my tummy!"
"Look Mum!" I shouted frantically,
"A unicorn with wind!"
"That's just Miss Tempest's little dog,"
She said to me, and grinned.

Snooping in the graveyard
In the lane beside the church,
Was a yeti, with spaghetti hair,
Sitting on a perch.
His funny face was twisted
In a weird and mournful way,
"I'm bored to death!" he moaned to me,
"Please will you come and play?"
"I'm sorry, Sir," I answered him,

"I'm going to school you see,
And yetis aren't allowed there
So you can't accompany me."
"Mum, Mum!" I cried. "A yeti, look!"
She said, "I will not bicker!
It's not a yeti, Mary,
You're just pointing at the vicar!"

By the gate at school,
I got another shocking fright,
I realised that my mother
Must have really bad eyesight.
She said a bright, "Good morning,"
To a horned and scaly creature,
The truth was out, without a doubt,
That was my head teacher!

Mary Eva Cottrell (8)
Helsby Hillside Primary School, Helsby

The Tooth Fairy Castle

The tooth fairy woke me in the middle of the night,
I was so scared, she gave me a fright.
Her name was Moonshine, she wanted me to see
Her castle in the forest that was waiting for me.
Onto her wings, I climbed for a ride,
Into the woods and up to the sky.
As soon as we landed, all I could see
Was a castle made of teeth, yippee!
The castle was magic and in order to enter,
You needed a password like tooth or denture.
"Abracadabra!" No, that wasn't it,
So I tried 'wibbly wobbly' and that was a hit!
The door opened and there in front of me
Were hundreds of fairies winking at me.
"Come on in, Amy, to our castle of teeth
But please don't tell other children,
It's a secret you must keep!"

Amy Martindale (8)
Helsby Hillside Primary School, Helsby

Me And My Strange Family!

My family is strange and you're going to see why...

My grandma is an alien librarian,
Selling lots of books.
She sells magic books, talking books, blank books
And any kind of book you can think of!

My grandad is a wizard,
Which means he's super strong.
He buys books from Grandma
But he is married to Nanny.

My nanny is a witch with a soft, black cat,
Putting spells on people, can you believe that?
She flies on her amazing broomstick with seats.

My dad is an elf,
He is small with a big heart.
He rides Flickermena with my mum
All around the world at the weekend.

My mum is a pixie,
Her hair is brown and silky
And her clothes are silky too!
She loves being with her family, especially me!

I have a pet dragon called Flickermena,
Flickermena is strange, she hunts for food for us,
Flickermena is house-trained and knows tricks!

My pet wolf is called Nala, who loves us,
She guards precious stuff,
She's even a burglar alarm!
She loves everything she has,
Even a potato salad with chicken!

I am a fairy called Isabella
And I am eight.
I love my family and my friends
And I love school as well,
And now you have met everybody!

Charis Catherine Bintliff (8)
Helsby Hillside Primary School, Helsby

Mucky Cookie

I had the strangest dream last night,
A cookie challenged me to a fight!
Made from chocolate and orange
He was the weirdest biscuit I ever did find!
I turned him down in the nicest possible way
Instead, I challenged him to a race
To give him a chance so he could get a pace
He gladly accepted without a second thought
And believed my lesson would be well taught
"The battle is yours to choose!"
I knew whatever the choice
He was bound to lose
"Swimming!" I shouted out
As he bounced with excitement
And waved his arms about.
I stripped down to my underwear
And set about my task
Knowing once he hit the water
It would be the cookie's last
Before I could shout,
"On your marks, get set, go!"

The cookie dived in and then
He screamed, "No! I'm getting wet!"
Down and down the soggy biscuit sank
As I stood laughing upon the water bank
You see, what the cheating, mucky cookie
Hadn't thought through
Was that as soon as he got into the water,
He'd be chocolate stew!

Alistair Stead (11)
Helsby Hillside Primary School, Helsby

Fortnite

We're flying on the bus, all a hundred of us,
I jumped out on my glider, now I'm a cloud rider.
I land in Tomato Temple, quiet and gentle,
I find some loot and a gun to shoot.
I run around for a bit, it's a good job I am fit,
I see another player, he looks like a boss,
If I win, I will do the floss!
He shoots and shoots so I build a base,
I don't want second place!
I reload my gun ready to fire,
Maybe I should have built a little higher.
I don't have any meds so I could be dead,
A storm is coming so I better get running.
I hurtle to the circle,
Me Vs him, and I am going to win!
The tension is high when the bullets fly,
I see a supply drop up high in the sky.
I run towards it but will I die?
Do I take the risk fast and steady?
I hope the players' guns aren't ready.
I run towards the supply drop,

I built around it so now I can stop.
I've got a grenade launcher, I shoot at him,
The bottom of his base broke and then I win!

Blake Williams (10)
Helsby Hillside Primary School, Helsby

Neve's Adventures

Did you hear about today?
A little fairy named Neve lost her way
She got locked out of Fairy Land
Not knowing which way to stand
Then Neve remembered she had friends
Who lived just around the bend
Neve hadn't seen them for six years or more
Or even quite a bit before
Neve found her friends
Lois and Bella were their names
They had lots of fun playing different games
They couldn't sleep when they went to bed
With exciting thoughts of what lies ahead
Twenty-four hours later, what a big sleep
They made it back to Fairy Land
They tugged and tugged on those double doors
It was like a game of tug of war
Finally, the double doors opened
"Hip hip hooray!"
The end of an exciting, fairy day.

Neve Jones (7)
Helsby Hillside Primary School, Helsby

The Magic Dragon

He stepped onto the stage,
Wild-eyed and not fazed.
The audience waited,
As the dragon levitated.
He played card tricks with an ace in his jaws,
And a four in his claws.
He breathed fire to melt spoons,
Accidentally setting alight a witch's broom!
He swung his gigantic tail,
And a girl vanished with a wail.
He lifted a wing, the girl appeared with a ting!
You could hear a pin drop,
As he dropped a rabbit with a plop,
From his hat for us all to see.
The curtains swooshed closed,
And everybody rose.
The sound of applause,
Along with the dragon's mighty roar!
Brought our evening to a close.
It was a wondrous night for all!

Grace Olivia Murphy (10)
Helsby Hillside Primary School, Helsby

In The Night

Looking through my window
Late one summer's night,
Peering through the hedges,
What an awesome sight!
One long, wet nose, two pointed ears
And a coat so smooth and bright.
Two beautiful eyes that I can see
Glistening in the moonlight,
The leaves are hiding his silhouette.
He looks so small but he is nobody's pet,
Swishing his long and bushy tail,
Using the dusk as a veil
To hide himself from human touch
But we all love him, oh so much.
The fox we see, now on his feet,
He turns and leaves to find something to eat.
The night brings out so many adventures!
Far too many for us to mention.

Maisie Holding (7)
Helsby Hillside Primary School, Helsby

My Team

M anchester City is my favourite team
A güero is my favourite goal scorer
N icolás Otamendi making tackles
C utting through defences is De Bruyne
H elping at the back is John Stones
E derson making amazing saves
S terling whipping in crosses
T aking on players is Leroy Sané
E liaquim Mangala winning headers
R iyad Mahrez showing his skills.

C hampions League is ours to win
I lkay Gündoan scoring worldies
T he stadium is called the Etihad
Y es, come on City!

Reece Harley Donnelly (8)
Helsby Hillside Primary School, Helsby

Alien Invasion

On a dark, cold, misty night
Through the trees, I saw a light
The light shot up into the skies
And danced around before my eyes
Suddenly, everything around me changed
And I was floating up to this crazy plane
Now I was in a room that was completely white
I saw this shadow shining in the light
As the shadow came near, the shadow grew tall
This being was an alien and he called himself Paul
His skin was green, his eyes were black
He spoke with his mind and ensured me that
He came in peace and travelled alone
This was not an invasion
He was just trying to get home.

Louie Nuttall (8)
Helsby Hillside Primary School, Helsby

No Rules!

Welcome to my poem,
All about no rules,
This would be ace,
And really cool.

We would have midnight feasts
With all of our friends
As long as it would never end.

No more cleaning,
No more chores,
Because as we know,
It makes us bored.

We could spend all of our pocket money
On anything we want,
Ice cream, sweets and lots of treats,
And wonderful things to eat.

Silliness and screaming,
Not the usual things you hear,
In the world of no rules,
Kids are allowed to drink dirty beer!

Emily Davies (8)
Helsby Hillside Primary School, Helsby

In My World

In my world, I would have a cookie as the moon
The sun would be a giant potato
And you would write with a spoon
In my world, dogs would talk
Everything would be free
And plants would be able to walk
In my world, Lego would be alive
It would be Christmas every day
And bees would not live in a hive
Wars would not happen
There would be peace and love
And money would fall from the sky above
Trees would not die
And everybody would be able to fly
In my world, it would be very peaceful
And everyone would be happy.

Jake Antony Thakur (8)
Helsby Hillside Primary School, Helsby

Marvellous Milk

My grandad, the dairy farmer
Milks his cows twice a day,
In the summer, he makes silage and hay
From the month of May up until September
So always remember milk is splendour
And we enjoy it every day.
It makes my bones stronger
And my legs grow longer.
Each year, I'm that bit taller, not smaller,
All because of Grandad's marvellous milk!
The milk is white and creamy
Have it warm and it'll send you dreamy.
Have it with cereal to start your day
The right way with my grandad's marvellous milk.

Tiana-Nicole Grant (7)
Helsby Hillside Primary School, Helsby

The Monster In My Closet

I thought I saw a monster
In my closet late last night,
I would look inside to prove it
But I might just get a fright!
His eyes were gleaming brightly
And his teeth were as sharp as knives,
His ears were very cat-like,
I wondered, *does he have nine lives?*
Now it's Monday morning,
I need to get my clothes,
I wonder, can he smell me coming
With his short and stubby nose?
I creep towards my closet,
I need to get my hat,
I open up the door to see
It's Smudgey, our pet cat!

Charlie Holding (9)
Helsby Hillside Primary School, Helsby

Unicorn Craziness

Unicorns here,
Unicorns there,
The unicorns have stripy, blue hair.

Unicorns in school,
Unicorns in the shop,
They're making a mess but they won't stop.

Unicorns up high,
Unicorns down low,
Unicorns everywhere,
I told you they're not slow!

Unicorns in the bathroom,
Unicorns in the sea,
You can tell that the unicorns really like being free.

Unicorns where it is hot,
Unicorns where it is cold,
If you believe in unicorns, you'll never grow old.

Imogen Marsden (8)
Helsby Hillside Primary School, Helsby

A Party On The Moon

I flew to the moon
Like a hot air balloon
Using the fairy wings on my back
When I got there, I saw lots of dancing astronauts
Cooking a BBQ of brightly-coloured candy
My sister Lucy was building a popcorn house
While she sat and ate a chocolate mouse
Soon I was ready to go home
Holding an ice cream cone
Topped with illuminous popping candy
When I got back home
I found myself in bed
With a big giant bump on my sore red head
But I loved my party on the moon
And I hope to go back there soon.

Daisy Buckthorpe (8)
Helsby Hillside Primary School, Helsby

The Barber's Chair

Sitting in the barber's chair
On the floor, there's lots of hair
Just for fun, he spins me around
Wow so fast, I hear a sound
In the mirror something strange I saw
The enormous, real-life dinosaur!
How is this possible what I've seen?
This must be the barber shop time machine!
Volcanoes, cavemen, wars being fought
Now the chair stops spinning, I'm nearly caught
Upon my return to reality, the barber is there too
He holds up the mirror
And says, "How's that for you?"

Harry James Wilson (8)
Helsby Hillside Primary School, Helsby

The Land Of Sweets

As I was polishing the giant candy cane,
I thought to myself, *I'm in the land of sweets!*
There are candy canes and chocolate planes,
Children writing with strawberry pencils,
Hershey's kisses to show their love,
Bowling with Maltesers on the playground,
Sherbet Dib Dabs for those who are cool,
Flying saucers to take you to school,
Smooth chocolate rivers and lollipop trees,
"What could be better?" I hear you say.
I'm off to the Land of No School to play!

Kaya Rose Howard (10)
Helsby Hillside Primary School, Helsby

The Fairy Land

Amongst the bluebells and snowdrops, we see
A little fairy who is making tea,
Sets a table with a cloth of silk,
And places a teapot next to the milk.

The cakes she is baking smells oh so grand
And they are the best in all the land.
The teacups are ready and waiting you see,
She is setting a place for Mr Bee.
Butterfly and Ladybird hear the party is ready.
They are spreading the word
Everyone is welcome! says the sign I see
She is even setting a place for me!

Tilly Axford (7)
Helsby Hillside Primary School, Helsby

The Magical Park Behind My House

Ssh listen, what's that sound?
Children laughing all around
Ssh listen, what's that sound?
The big circus is here and loud
Ssh listen, what's that sound?
Candyfloss bushes all around
Ssh listen, what's that sound?
Dancing gummy bears for a pound
Ssh listen, what's that sound?
Strawberry laces swirling in the fairground
Ssh listen, what's that sound?
Me jumping off the giant mound
And splashing in pools of orange Fanta
Feeling very proud.

Lewis Stanley Plant (8)
Helsby Hillside Primary School, Helsby

I'm Going To Get You

As I swam softly counting one, two, three
I came across this big, huge creature staring at me
My tummy started to moan, I think I needed lunch
I wondered what would happen
If I just had a munch
But fish don't eat sharks
Although he did look scrummy
The shark turned around and cried for his mummy
My teeth opened wide, my mouth slammed shut
And all that was left were bones from his butt!
Fish don't eat sharks so they say
But look what happened here today.

Emma O'Hanlon (7)
Helsby Hillside Primary School, Helsby

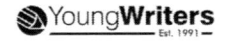

The Tangled-Up Octopus

Once, there was an octopus who lived in a cave,
But he wanted to be brave.
The problem with this octopus was
When he came upon an enemy,
He always shivered in the icy sea.
This octopus always tried his best
But it always ended in a tangled mess.
He had to call his mates,
It was always great,
But this time, his mate got stuck in his tentacles!
They called his shark friend
But this time, he had tricked them,
Instead of helping them,
He ate them up!

Emily Lightfoot (7)
Helsby Hillside Primary School, Helsby

To Sail Around The World

The speedboat's ready
It is time to go
What I will see
I do not know
I set off excited
The jet fuel ignited
Faster than sound
I speed around
Across oceans and seas
Feeling the breeze
Africa, Asia, America and Europe
I really can't afford a hold-up
Around the world in a day
Seagulls show me the way
The end is in sight
Sun shining bright
Ran out of fuel
But it was so cool!

Sam Mozeley (10)
Helsby Hillside Primary School, Helsby

The Goblins In The Big City

There are goblins hiding
A big city they are finding
A road lined with trees
Scattered with autumn leaves
The city is soon in sight
Into houses, the goblins will fight
Tomato sauce is what they're after
They like to graffiti with it right up to the rafter
Once the goblins mission is complete
There are hot dogs and burgers for all to eat
After all, they only wanted tomato sauce
To go with their treat.

Conor Hayes (8)
Helsby Hillside Primary School, Helsby

Ladder In The Sky

Step by step, I climbed the ladder
Beneath me, Mother was getting madder!

I reached the top and I could see
A magical world before me!

With candyfloss clouds and lollipop trees
Sweet-smelling stardust blowing in the breeze

A chocolate palace glistened in the sun
Oh to live here would be so much fun!

But then I heard my mother call my name
I must go now before she goes insane!

Anabel Porter (10)
Helsby Hillside Primary School, Helsby

Music And Me

I love to play music
I love to play the guitar
It makes me feel like a pop star

I love to play music
I love to play my piano
I love to play the notes high and low

I love to play music
I love to play my trumpet
I am learning to play the best music hits

I love to play my instruments
I would love to learn more
Come and join me too
Because music is fun for me and you!

Heidi Edwards (8)
Helsby Hillside Primary School, Helsby

The Space Race

I travelled up to space,
You should've seen my face!
I shot up in my rocket,
Eating cake out of my pocket.
When I arrived there,
I ate my juicy pear.
I watched an alien race,
One was driving really ace.
The red car was in the lead,
Going at top speed.
The posh car won first-place,
What a super smashing race!
On Earth, I landed with a bump
And did a loud trump!

Noah George Morphet (7)
Helsby Hillside Primary School, Helsby

To Destroy A Planet

A bad alien came to destroy Jupiter
He was very small and green
He flew in a big, silver spaceship
This alien was really, really mean
He had special wind power
Which came out of his hands
He flew all the way to the planet
And hit the planet with a bang
The police were trying to save it
They were throwing rocks at him
They hit him on the head
And threw him in the bin.

Mathieu Fell (7)
Helsby Hillside Primary School, Helsby

Grog The Fox

I fell down but I didn't pull a frown,
I landed on the ground with only one pound.
I went to the shops and bought a fox
That wore four socks and came in a box.
I named him Grog
And he loved to play with a log.
Green is my favourite colour
And a dog is my favourite pet
So I put them together and it made a good name!
Then I went to the vet
So she could see my new pet.

Heidi Fleming (7)
Helsby Hillside Primary School, Helsby

When My Cat Could Talk

Rosie is my cat's name
Sometimes we play a little game
She can be crazy and loves to play
We do it almost every day

I heard a funny sound
And my heart began to pound
The noise came from near my cat
I went over to give her a little pat

She tickled my lips
As I gave her a kiss
She really did surprise me
By saying, "I need a wee!"

Amelia White (7)
Helsby Hillside Primary School, Helsby

Underwater Football

Underwater football
The game I know so well
But don't try to play it
When the water starts to swell
The swordfish struggles with his long, spiky nose
But he keeps the opposition on their toes!
Five minutes until full time
The score is nil-nil
But who's this coming with his super gill?
Wait, here comes the fast school
To score the winning goal!

Charlie Jackson (8)
Helsby Hillside Primary School, Helsby

The Invisibility Cloak

One day, I found the invisibility cloak
I spotted it near a big rock
I put it on and didn't go to school
'Cause I felt really, really cool
Instead, I went to Chester Zoo
And sat next to a kangaroo
I had decided to travel the world
I even got to Greenland, but it was too cold
The day had come to an end
It was great, so I lent the cloak to my friend.

Oscar Satur (10)
Helsby Hillside Primary School, Helsby

Candy World

The dragons speak
While I quickly eat a house full of sweets
While we eat, the dragons sleep day and night
When they awaken
They fly and fly like never before
In this world, dragons go to school
And learn to eat candy politely
While we sleep, dragons are giving lifts to people
In this world, there is one thing that isn't candy
And that is Christmas!

Cerys Rogers (10)
Helsby Hillside Primary School, Helsby

A Pocket Full Of Candy

A pocket full of candy, one, two, three
A secret place for you and me
A rumbling, a tumbling, what could it be?
Grab your coats and rush outside
Percy's exploding far and wide!
Delicious, popping candy, no time to hide
Pink and yellow lava lies around
Children scoop the treasure from the ground
Our pockets bulge with what we've found.

Ava Rose Pollard (9)
Helsby Hillside Primary School, Helsby

Camel Chaos

Watching camels sweeping by
Over our heads, there they fly
One by one we all follow
Observing them eating swallows
Gliding down to drink some water
I don't know how she learnt to fly
Or who taught her
Oh, I wish I could ride on a camel's back
Through the oceans, the mountains too
Oh, I wish I could ride on a camel's back!

Nancy Farmer (10)
Helsby Hillside Primary School, Helsby

WWE Under The Sea

Welcome to WWE under the sea
On the left rock pool, we have Lewis the lionfish
He's big, mean, what a monster machine!
On the right rock pool, we have Rocky Coral
Ready to wrestle, ready to rumble
Through the sandy water they tumble
The crowd goes wild to watch their winner
Before they get eaten by a great white shark for his dinner.

Louie Joseph Burns (9)
Helsby Hillside Primary School, Helsby

Crazy World

While I was on a boat, I fell asleep
I dreamt that Lego was jumping with glitter on it
How exciting my dream was
I was very, very happy
My pen was running red
The glass was going crazy
I made a potion
It was the best potion of all
Because the potion was powerful!
It made me excited...
This crazy world that I was in.

Bailey Sidney Kaye (7)
Helsby Hillside Primary School, Helsby

The Wolf

Beautiful, proud, waiting, observing...
A predator walking in the shadows
He raises his muzzle to the bright full moon
He howls his lonely song
The call of the wild
Blazing fire eyes, hardly tame
You take one look and you run
But the pitch-black fur, it fades away in the night
But all you can see is his golden fire eyes.

Lei Perry (10)
Helsby Hillside Primary School, Helsby

Countries, Places And Things

As the map lay there
Looking very white and bare
It suddenly glowed with light
And then I jumped back in fright

It talked to me about trees
And bees and not to mention
My poor knees!
Also a house
And a mouse
And England
And then Finland
That is what the map said
After that, I went back to bed.

Oscar Walton (8)
Helsby Hillside Primary School, Helsby

Not Again

I think I need more practice
When jumping on a cactus
Because it really kind of sucks
My dad shook his bum
And walked towards the cactus
He tripped over and fell face-first
Me and my mum laughed
My dad was not happy
I shook my bum at him
And laughed even more than before
We wouldn't be doing that again!

Archie Coyne (7)
Helsby Hillside Primary School, Helsby

Dancing On The Stars

I'm up high in the sky on a beautiful night
I dance around the stars
They twinkle with delight
I twirl, leap and spin
I do this with a grin
No one would believe where I've been
As I float slowly down to land
The stars give me a helping hand
Blinking stars shine bright
Oh, what a beautiful sight!

Paige Olivia Cowper (7)
Helsby Hillside Primary School, Helsby

A Fairy Wish

I wish I was a fairy
With wings fluttery and light
I'd fly among the clouds
Sprinkling stardust at night

I'd sit among the flowers
Thinking up dreams so wonderful and bright
To share with the children
As they slept tight
What a wonderful thing it would be
To be a fairy spreading glee.

Zoe Jade Littler (7)
Helsby Hillside Primary School, Helsby

Lollipop

In the land of sweets and candy
Where the sugar monster lives
There are some dancing lollipops
They are very creative
They dance around the chocolate lake
And up in the candyfloss trees
They smell so sweet
And attract the honey bees
The dancing lollipops bop
Until they go *pop!*

Chiara Autumn Ferraro-Smith (7)
Helsby Hillside Primary School, Helsby

Unicorn Fish

Deep in the ocean
At the bottom of the sea
There's a unicorn fish
Who is waving at me
He's green, yellow, purple and blue
He swims to me and says, "How do you do?"
He rides the waves until he loses the light
And says goodbye to the day
And hello to the night.

Brooke McBride (10)
Helsby Hillside Primary School, Helsby

Carrying A Bus

I carry a bus
As you can see
My face will fill with anxiety
As I make the bus go up
I am filled with surprise
As people fill my hat with money
I drop the bus carefully
And get some more money
I will share, it's not just mine
I will give to everyone!

Nooralhoda Al-Zubaidy (10)
Helsby Hillside Primary School, Helsby

The Crazy Circus

Red lions are dancing everywhere
Tarantulas are crawling out of my hair
A panda in a blue jumper is wrestling a koala
Polar bears are doing gymnastics
And they are very enthusiastic
And a very cool skateboarding rabbit
Is trying to give up his terrible habit.

Willow Walton (8)
Helsby Hillside Primary School, Helsby

Meatballs Of Fire

I am the meatball man
I grew up in a meatball can
I really did, I'm not a liar
I like them really hot so I breathe fire
I am the meatball robber
And I'll take them off your plate
But I'll promise to share them with you
If you are my mate.

Luca Mark-Aroon Singh (7)
Helsby Hillside Primary School, Helsby

Alien Talk

I had a dream
I went to the moon
I saw an alien
One or two
One was big
Two were small
They said, "Beep boopla!"
I said, "Beep bla?"
I woke up the next day
With shivers on my back
I'd learnt how to talk alien!

Rose Slator (9)
Helsby Hillside Primary School, Helsby

Oceans And Lands

The oceans and lands sometimes have stories
Oceans and lands are sometimes gory
But we need them both to survive
Even though they can't revive
We need to help the land
We need to help the ocean
We need to stop all of the pollution.

Aleesa Pynadath (8)
Helsby Hillside Primary School, Helsby

My Alicorn Dream

In my dreams, I ride an alicorn
With a purple mane and a silver horn
Her voice is so sweet, she almost sings
She has amazing, dazzled, feathered wings
Then I wake from my sleep
Eyes closed tight, my dreams to keep.

Mia Skarnes (8)
Helsby Hillside Primary School, Helsby

The Clown

A clown chased me down the street
So I bit him and he bit me
He chased me here
He chased me there
He chased me everywhere!

Jacob Green (7)
Helsby Hillside Primary School, Helsby

Eagle Snoring

I climbed a tree to find a nest
I found an eagle in its vest
I found this rather boring
He just lay there loudly snoring!

Anthony Davidson (7)
Helsby Hillside Primary School, Helsby

My Tree House Unicorn

My tree house unicorn has magic powers
She can make Christmas snow with her horn
When you ride her, your dreams can come true
When she swishes her tail
She does a unicorn poop
It looks like popcorn
And it tastes like it too!

Maisie Jayne Hall (10)
Ladywood School & Outreach Service, Little Lever

Cute Alice

Alice is kind
Alice is friendly
Alice is funny
And puts fish in jelly
Alice is cute
Alice is hilarious
Alice makes beds from crisps!

Casey Booth (10)
Ladywood School & Outreach Service, Little Lever

Silly Land

In Silly Land...
Animals live there
Elephants and monkeys
There are trees with apples
Silly Land is good!

Thomas Edge (8)
Ladywood School & Outreach Service, Little Lever

Happy Land

My school is happy
The teachers are nice
Learning is good
Playtime is fun
My school is the best!

Marcus Buckley (8)
Ladywood School & Outreach Service, Little Lever

The Terrible Torture Upon London

We squabble through the muddy meadows,
Although not the very best time,
Not a tiny speck of yellow,
What he's doing is such a crime.

To set our beloved London on fire
Was not their desire,
But to the poor Jews,
That was just old news.

Our beloved bodies of friends
Scattered everywhere,
England, London was just
Their blood-soaked funfair.
We were all promised something
We would not get,
And since the war started,
Death was destined to be met.

Vareen Hussain
Meanwood Community Nursery & Primary School, Rochdale

Blue

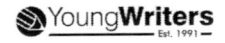

Blue is the look of a shiny mermaid's tail
In the cold, wet sea.
It is the small, juicy blueberry
Exploding in my mouth.
It is also the feel of a unicorn's silky, smooth hair.
It is like the cold, icy breath of a snow monster.
It is the swooping of a little bluebird in the sky.
It is the small toy car in the middle of a race.
It is like a butterfly gathering nectar
On a dark night.
Blue is a beautiful, velvety dress
Being worn to a party.

Evie Morris (8)
Old Hall Primary School, Brandlesholme

Blue

Blue is a stomp from Godzilla
And the taste of bubblegum topping vanilla
It looks like a phoenix's tail
And an elegant sea monster's scales
It sounds like the sea singing a gentle song
There's a magnificent mermaid
Swimming all day long
It feels like a soft carpet beneath my feet
And sounds like a bluetit's tweet
Blue tastes like a slushy waiting to be drank
By me and a lollipop as stick as can be.

Noah Budgen (8)
Old Hall Primary School, Brandlesholme

Blue

Blue is the colour of a deadly Siren
Dragging sailors to their deaths
It is icy dragon breath
It is a silky unicorn's mane flying through the air
It is the sticky slime covering my hair
It is the fluffy feathers on a phoenix
Hunting for its prey
It is the eye on a Cyclops in the middle of the day
It is the scaly skin of a mermaid
Swimming in the ocean.

Daniel Taylor (9)
Old Hall Primary School, Brandlesholme

Moon Cow Mayhem

Standing in a field is a scaly llama man
Squash! Squash! Squash!
Squeezing out are slimy moon cows
Slop! Slop! Spill! Spill!
So many moon cows come spilling out
Standing in a field of moon cows
Frightens llama man...
Squish! Squish! Squash! Squash!
Squashed by a herd of moon cows.

Charlie Collinge (8)
Old Hall Primary School, Brandlesholme

Green

Green is the ribbit of a frog bouncing in the grass
It is as beautiful as unicorn's mane
It is a leprechaun's hat
And as impeccable as a dragon's scales
It is the taste of sour slime
And as lovely as the summer leaves
Hanging on the trees
Green is a bogey falling out of an ogre's nose!

Ava Waterhouse (8)
Old Hall Primary School, Brandlesholme

Blue

Blue is a huge humpback whale
It's the feathers of a small quail
It's the curl of a swirling tsunami
A glance of the aqua, shining sea
It's also crayons doing a great drawing
It is a bluebell magically blooming
Blue is a big, bouncy ball
It's a sky with no clouds at all!

Charlie O'Hara (9)
Old Hall Primary School, Brandlesholme

Wonder

W onderful whales waving through the window
O ctopus in the ocean eating oranges
N injas never wear their suits at night
D inosaurs doing dances in a deep, dark dungeon
E lephants eating everything every day
R abbits robbing robots and running really fast.

Brodie Keenan (8)
Old Hall Primary School, Brandlesholme

Green

Green is a leprechaun's hat
It is as rough as a dragon's scales
And like the roar of a dragon
It is when sweet apples blow off trees
Green is as smooth as a mermaid's tail
And like parrots' feathers on your face
Green is an ogre's trump!

Jack Brooks (8)
Old Hall Primary School, Brandlesholme

Blue

Blue is a bright blue lake
That feels like a soft, sweet blueberry
Blue is a blue pan that sizzles like a witch's potion
It is as blue as the sky like a Cyclops' eye
It is as fuzzy as a teddy bear
Blue is the deep ocean.

Eva Smith (8)
Old Hall Primary School, Brandlesholme

Riding Around A Rainbow

I'm riding on a rainbow
With some very strange dogs,
They bark about not having their fluffy shark.
It is not real but good luck if you own one,
That thing on its back is not a cone!
My dogs are very strange,
They have three heads each
And some of them are peach!
You will try finding these dogs,
Just kidding, they don't bark,
They are three-headed toy teddies!
The rainbow smells of unicorns
And it looks like I'm going to fall
Because the rainbow is nearly complete
And they call the ride the very colourful rainbow!

Emily Turpin (8)
St Aidan's RC Primary School, Ashington

Fairycorn Land

Fairycorn Land, where they walk and also talk
The fairies are looking at me
So I say, "Will you please stop looking at me?"
But when I walk, I see the unicorns
Spitting glitter at me!
When I am looking
I see the tea spout cooking
I would like a cup of tea
But then we play hide-and-seek
I take a peek, then I fall asleep
I see some sheep as they leap.

Lexi Hedley (8)
St Aidan's RC Primary School, Ashington

Black

Black is a dark colour
As dark as a wintery night
With a blow of wind
The black night makes a fright
But the colour black has a bit of might
The colour black is like the rain
Black is like a complete forest
Black is as dark as the night's sky
Black is dark and it is a thunderstorm
Black makes it dark and scary
The colour black gives me a fright.

Jireh Eunice Lagmay (6)
St Aidan's RC Primary School, Ashington

Wind In The Willows

The wind is blowing
The leaves are growing
The birds are singing
The mice are creeping
The owls are hooting
The squirrels are shooting
The hedgehogs scurry
The rabbits hurry
The deer are galloping
The wind stops howling
And all is quiet and peaceful
And all the animals are asleep
And will wake up to be joyful.

Savannah White (8)
St Aidan's RC Primary School, Ashington

Guess The Colour

This colour is so beautiful
Like the glimmering, glowing sea.
The sun lies deeply in this thing.
This colour is very popular and we are wearing it.
It can be dark and light
And it's my favourite colour.
It is like the shining sky on a summer's day.
It is the deep ocean.
What colour is it?

Answer: Blue.

Evie Biswell (7)
St Aidan's RC Primary School, Ashington

Magical

The children are so happy
So happy at Christmas
The breeze is so cold
It is as cold as ice!
The sky is like the sun, so bright
The storm is coming
Here come the burning flames in the fireplace
There's a vicious lion and a queen bee
The wind is as fast as a cheetah
And the sun shines brightly in my eyes.

Lewis Ligtley (7)
St Aidan's RC Primary School, Ashington

Red And Blue

Red looks like a beautiful rose
Red smells like a steamy fire
Red sounds like a robin singing
Red feels like an autumn leaf
Red tastes like a strawberry lolly

Blue is the sea
Blue is the colourful mind
Blue is a clear sky
Blue is quiet and peaceful
Blue is the beads on my bowl.

Emily Louise Richardson (7)
St Aidan's RC Primary School, Ashington

Guess The Colour

This colour is beautiful like the glimmering sun
The sun lies deeply in this colour
This colour is very, very popular
It can be dark or light
It is also my favourite colour
It is like the sky on a summery day
It is like the deep ocean
What colour is it?

Answer: Blue.

Narisara Fletcher (7)
St Aidan's RC Primary School, Ashington

Banana, Banana

I danced with a banana
And he did the cha-cha
But I did the waltz
He got it wrong
I guided him through
When he left, I was all alone
Then I saw him and proposed
He said, "I do!"
We danced all night long
And we both got it wrong
But we didn't care.

Eva Scott (7)
St Aidan's RC Primary School, Ashington

The Monster Burps Goo

There is a monster named Blam
He burps goo that looks like a clam
It is horrible and sticky
He is very picky
He doesn't like to take
But he likes gooey cake!
Oh dear, I didn't think I was going to fear
What a mess!
I need a rest
This has gone terribly wrong!

Lily Williamson (7)
St Aidan's RC Primary School, Ashington

White

White is like a feather
White is like silence
White is like a plane's colour
White is the taste of marshmallows
White is the colour of snow
White is the colour of paper
White smells plain
White is the colour of a rubber
White is light like a whiteboard.

Mya Teasdale (7)
St Aidan's RC Primary School, Ashington

Red

Red is as red as a car
Red is as red as blood
Red is as red as paint
Red is as red as a poppy
Red is as red as a rose
Red is as red as a Chinese lantern
Red is as red as a strawberry
Red is as red as a cherry
As red as a tomato
And as red as red hot.

Nathan Catania (7)
St Aidan's RC Primary School, Ashington

Blue

Blue is a beautiful waterfall
Blue is rain falling from a cloud
Blue is the sky
Blue is the colour that I like the best
Blue is the colour of the oceans
Blue is the colour of the seas
Blue is the colour of some cardigans
Blue is the colour of blueberries.

Lilly Slater (7)
St Aidan's RC Primary School, Ashington

Guess The Colour

It is the colour of the grass
It is the colour of a pencil
It is the colour of the stems for flowers
It is as bright as the sun reflecting on the grass
It is a high tree where the birds make nests
What colour is it?

Answer: Green.

Lillani Grace McBride (7)
St Aidan's RC Primary School, Ashington

Black

Black is the monster
Black is dark
Black is the feeling of sadness
Black is the colour of a burnt marshmallow
Black darkness makes people scared
Black is the colour of hair
Black is the sound of thunder
Black is the night-time monster.

Franchesca Santos (7)
St Aidan's RC Primary School, Ashington

Guess The Colour

It is a tall bushy tree
It is the stem of a flower
It is bright like the sky
It is the colour of a burger ingredient
It is a good food colour
It is the colour of candy
What colour is it?

Answer: Green.

Jake Wheldon (7)
St Aidan's RC Primary School, Ashington

Sweety Land

Sweets, so many sweets!
To eat, to crunch
The lollies are red
The bubblegum is blue
The chewy snacks are sour
Tasty Skittles are as bright as the sun
There are lots of flavours coming to you
From Sweety Land!

Harry Robson (8)
St Aidan's RC Primary School, Ashington

A Dragon For A Pet

You don't want a dragon for a pet
Because it's slippery and slimy
And it doesn't stay, it wiggles
Its favourite food is chocolate
So don't leave any anywhere
Or the dragon might pay you a visit!

Charlie Mazzella (8)
St Aidan's RC Primary School, Ashington

The Colour Pink!

Pink is as shiny as gold pearls and diamonds
Pink is the colour in the rainbow
Pink shines like a heart
Pink is the colour of an ear
Pink is the evening sky
Pink makes me feel happy like two marshmallows!

Evie Grace French (6)
St Aidan's RC Primary School, Ashington

The Magic Crisp

The magic crisp flies so high
It gives me a ride in the sky
Up above the clouds
I look across at the blue amazing, awesome sky
It takes me to space to see Mercury, Venus, Earth
And all the planets!

Jaden Tait (8)
St Aidan's RC Primary School, Ashington

Guess The Colour

The stars shine like a diamond
It shines brighter than the stars and the sun
It is so bright, I can't believe its colour!
Will it be gold, yellow, purple
Or will it be brown or red?

Abbie Vout (7)
St Aidan's RC Primary School, Ashington

Red

Red looks like a beautiful rose
Red smells like the steamy fire
Red sounds like a robin singing
Red feels like the autumn leaves
Red tastes like a strawberry lolly.

Olivia Hewitt (7)
St Aidan's RC Primary School, Ashington

Blue

Blue is as clear as a river moving
And water from the sea
Blue is a shark chomping in the water
Blue is the sky
And my colour eyes.

Jack Robert Patrick Jarvis (8)
St Aidan's RC Primary School, Ashington

The Hamburger

The hamburger is the best,
But it is served with fries,
The hardest thing to theft,
And then everybody cries.

It is served with two buns,
And in the middle, a patty,
With lots of sums,
Lettuce makes people happy!

The cheese is great,
And tomatoes are good,
I'd put on a cape,
And make some food!

I hope you come after,
There's a grill to mend,
We had lots of laughter,
And that's not the end.

Our neighbour is bad,
But his restaurant is made of logs,

While that's sad,
People now like hot dogs!

Our neighbour is lucky,
He has a recipe,
He'll get a puppy,
And roast it for me!

The people got sick,
And he lost his money,
Now we can take the mick,
And that's funny!

Oliver Gracia-Ruiz (8)
St Catherine's RC Primary School, Sandyford

Space Sharks

Space sharks live in craters on the moon
Their furniture is the size of a spoon

They eat aliens for breakfast, tea and lunch
From 5000 miles away, all you can hear is crunch

They wear blue alien skin
They throw light green ones in the bin

They have 7,000 eyes
They are like professional spies

Their heads look like burger buns
But unfortunately, they're scared of humans

They have long tails
If I measured them
It would be the size of 9,000 whales

They have ten heads
They are all multicoloured but mostly red.

Qasim Akhtar (8)
St Catherine's RC Primary School, Sandyford

In The Great Fire Of London

Run away, run away, your house is on fire,
The smoke is getting higher,
Smoke is in the air,
So don't even think about getting a pear.

Be careful you don't die,
If someone made some apple pie,
I wouldn't try any at all.
Suddenly I met a man called Paul.

Paul loved dancing at the ball,
I liked skipping with Paul,
I thought he was a nice man,
But he robbed my money and fell in the well.

The fire kept on going,
I felt very scared, the fire was glowing,
But in the end, the fire stopped,
The fire had come to an end.

Amir Orand (8)
St Catherine's RC Primary School, Sandyford

The Cool Gang

A unicorn on a skateboard
Riding down a hill of doors!
A clock is hitting a dog bone on a hill!
Advancing Fork dancing on the head of Mr Bell

Then they had a party and played Twister
With Mr Bill, everyone was excited
Then Unicorn Sparkle had
A skateboard competition
And she won!

They had a pool party and swam
And they flew up in the sky
Then splashed into the pool

The cool gang watched clocks
Having a knitting competition
And she won a trophy
Fork had a dance performance
And won
That's the cool gang.

Chloe Logue (9)
St Catherine's RC Primary School, Sandyford

The Animal Hospital

There were once hospitals,
That were run by animals.
Dragons, sheep, goats and hens,
But it really depends
If you like animals,
In hospitals.

Once there were some men
That were looked after by a hen.
One of the men had broken his leg,
And had begun to beg
For the hospital nurse
To give him some of the contents of her purse.

But he was not the first
To ask for the contents of her purse,
To ask for the contents of her purse.
More unfortunate news,
An ice cream space rock hit the hospital.
That was the end of that.

Sarah Humphrey (8)
St Catherine's RC Primary School, Sandyford

Food

When you see it your mouth waters,
When I'm in a bad mood I look at my food posters,
You can find it in the south,

It runs down the block,
And hides behind a rock,
When their enemies see it,
They can't stop looking at it,

It's so delicious you can't stop eating it,
You can exercise with it,
It can be healthy,
It can be greasy,

My best friend is allergic to it,
So he ends up eating rocks,
Even aliens have it, it's so good,
I found someone eating it in the mud.

Grace Emily Dixon (9)
St Catherine's RC Primary School, Sandyford

Watermelon Palace Party

The watermelon goes to eat,
But there is no seat!
Going to explore,
Opening the magic door!

Want to play with the piñata
See a girl called Marta!
Don't know what to do,
Say to the fly, "Shoo!"

Watermelon is super happy,
See a fast bunny!
Find a teleporting circle with a candy cane,
Go through it and hear a gurgle down the drain!

Teleports me to the sea,
Watermelon finds a key!
See a great big fin,
Find a smelly bin!

Mariya Z Wasif (8)
St Catherine's RC Primary School, Sandyford

The Transforming Beach

A man went to the beach,
He had a great day.
There was no sea,
It rained at the bay.

He was so sad,
He got all wet.
The sun came out,
It made him so upset.

But then it turned cold,
The sand went white.
The wind made him bald,
Then he got frostbite.

It was winter,
The man got his buddies.
They went on snowboards,
Then had lunch and it was yummy.

Neghot Abrehe (9)
St Catherine's RC Primary School, Sandyford

Trampolining Circus

Lions doing backflips,
Slithering snakes showing their tactics,
Puppies dancing,
Zebras prancing.

Rhinos bouncing on their tail,
Bunnies swinging, then away they sail,
Elephants hanging on the roof,
They let go and hoot.

Monkeys being cheeky,
Giraffes looking sleepy,
Crazy circus snacks put a smile on your face,
All the animals make the tent a great place.

Theo Robertson (8)
St Catherine's RC Primary School, Sandyford

On The Beach

Swimming in the sea,
Eating a pea,
Finding shells,
Digging big wells.

Catching a huge crab,
And then I dab,
Surfing on the waves,
Searching the caves.

Wearing swimming suits,
Kicking off your boots,
Building sandcastles,
Eating Fruit Pastels.

Swimming with the dolphins,
I see Mary Poppins,
Riding a turtle,
Oh! I love purple.

Anna Carr (8)
St Catherine's RC Primary School, Sandyford

A Great World

In my own world,
I'd like my house to be made of chocolate.
In swimming, I'd like an invisible locket.

In the world, I'd like a talking cupcake.
We could go on a brilliant rainbow lake.

The moon made out of yellow cheese
I wouldn't like any of those nasty fleas

The pizza man made out of delicious pizza
What a nice feature!

Nikki Garcia Kukilo (9)
St Catherine's RC Primary School, Sandyford

Dancing In A Pineapple

A girl that's dancing in a pineapple
She always dances like a ballerina

She really loves dancing in a pineapple
Because she likes pineapples and dancing

She dances so well that people come to watch

She has a performance every Friday
She plays dancing games sometimes
She dances so beautifully people clap
Every day and every night.

Maisie Francis (8)
St Catherine's RC Primary School, Sandyford

Candy Chaos

It was a normal day at Candy Land
People were walking up and down the streets
Sweets started to rain heavily
And caramel bars were raining down on Candy Land.

All of a sudden,
Cookie aliens were invading the planet
And getting their pocket money!
The fizzy pop stars were exploding
Later, when the aliens left,
Everyone went to rebuild.

Matthew Morley (8)
St Catherine's RC Primary School, Sandyford

Swimming Animals

First, all the animals dive into the tank,
The sea lions doing backflips,
The tigers showing all of their tactics,
The puppies front somersault against the wall,

The bunnies hop and jump through hoops,
After that, the kittens loop.
Finally, food falls from the sky,
Delicious, yummy mice pies.

Karen Shi (8)
St Catherine's RC Primary School, Sandyford

Underwater School

As brave as Trevor
A person that never stops talking
As mean as a teacher
As silly as a creature

As crazy as a party
As amazing as karate
As silent as a wall
As loud as a mall

As clumsy as a bug
As filled as a jug
As tiny as a mouse
As huge as a house.

Charlie Crass (8)
St Catherine's RC Primary School, Sandyford

The Day I Disappeared...

As I got sucked in,
My thumb was struck with a pin.
As I screamed, "Let me out!"
My mum began to scream and shout.

I banged and banged, "Help me now!"
I tripped over, "Argh, ow!"
Do you see how hard it can be?
I couldn't even see!

"Oh sorry, sorry, let me out,"
I began to scream and shout.
When I started to wander around,
I couldn't even feel the ground.

Then I noticed I was there,
In the console, playing with a bear.
He had spiky, brown hair,
Though I could see him, was I really there?!

Ewan Anthony Blud (9)
St Mary's Catholic Primary School, Crewe

Lottery Love

I once won the lottery
At least 900 grand
The money just kept rolling in
Coming in a van.

At first, I bought a brand new house
Several hundred miles wide
I gave it new accessories
Like a giant water slide.

There was a shiny bike I liked
So I told my mum to buy it
And all my friends adored my money
So I had to hide it.

And then at sixteen, I chose to gamble
I gave my money to betting folk
They started to ramble
And then I was broke.

Theresa Cross (10)
St Mary's Catholic Primary School, Crewe

A Goddess' Quest

I lifted Zeus' sword
And picked up Hera's shield
The dragon snored
As I ran across the field.

I pierced its underbelly
The first task was complete
But now I had to eat camel jelly
Using only my teeny feet!

With two tasks done
I had nothing to fear
Except to have fun
Without killing the deer!

I sat on my throne looking gorgeous
Feeling utter happiness and contentedness
For I was in Mount Olympus
I was now a wise goddess.

Layla Finney (9)
St Mary's Catholic Primary School, Crewe

The School Of Nightmares

Children have nightmares, right?
Well, now it is time to give you a fright
Zombies, dinosaurs, skeletons and witches
And giants that are the size of twenty pitches
The books are all covered in blood
And monsters think that is good
But the witches always ignore
While zombies mostly snore
Every monster yawns
When it is about to turn to dawn.

Sophie Holly-Marie Cherrington (10)
St Mary's Catholic Primary School, Crewe

Guinea Pig Horror

Once I got a guinea pig
It was cute, furry but big
I picked it up and it bit me
"Ouch, ouch, ouch!"
The next day, I got up
And found it on my couch!

Up in his hutch, it smelt so bad
My mum fainted and it made my little brother sad
I found him chewing an old, grubby pen
After I found his pooey den!

He ate horrible, rotten cauliflower
After a week, I found out he had superpowers
I must say, never, ever have a guinea pig!

Eline Streefkerk (9)
The Firs School, Chester

The Dragon Wants To Be A Sheep

Once, there was a dragon big and strong,
Also, there was a sheep who did magic wrong.
The sheep ate rice and the dragon ate flowers,
The dragon tried to get the silly sheep's powers!
So once the sheep had gone to sleep,
The naughty dragon did a leap.
He jumped on top of the sheep
And took his powers without moving a peep.
Now the dragon is not just big and strong,
He sounds like a sheep and it's just so wrong!

Frankie (8)
The Firs School, Chester

Crazy Vegetables

V elvet carrots running mad,
E ggy kale feeling very sad.
G reen lettuce not very well,
E nergetic sprouts slipping and ringing a bell.
T acky chillies all worked up,
A bel the celery saying, "What's up?"
B ubbly peppers feeling excited,
L ong cucumbers being united.
E normous potatoes really bright,
S ad turnips in the dark of night.

Thomas Bartley (8)
The Firs School, Chester

The Queen Is A Chocolate Bar!

The British queen is a chocolate bar,
Big, gooey and brown
And on her chocolate body
Sits a very chocolatey crown.

She could melt out in the sunshine
So the guards keep her inside.
The public wants to eat her
So in her palace, she must hide.

She never likes others to eat chocolate
So she banned it from day one.
It's always sad in Britain now
Because the yummy chocolate is gone.

Seb Wilson (8)
The Firs School, Chester

Where, Oh Where Is My Cat?

I have a cat and she is lost,
I don't want to get a new one,
I don't know how much it'll cost!
Apparently, she went to the moon
And then got caught up in a lagoon.
She went in an underwater lair
And she never did even care.
Then she met a sparkling unicorn
That was eating grass on the lawn.
From then on, my cat lived on the moon,
I never saw her again,
Oh cat, come home soon.

Eliza Turner (8)
The Firs School, Chester

Alien Holiday Invasion

I was going on holiday
I was going to surf by the bay
But before I could get on the aeroplane
Some aliens took me away!
They took me to their planet, Merth
And then I prayed to go back to Earth
But I stumbled around the tilted rock
And gave their spaceship a little knock
I hopped into their spaceship
And hoped I would make it
I drove their ship through space
They were annoyed I took it!

Zara Bickerstaff (8)
The Firs School, Chester

Dancing Tree

When I went to school, I saw a giant tree
Then my little dog did a colossal wee!
The big tree started to do a dance
Next, it bashed and banged and began to prance.

The tree's dancing was very weird
Then it grew a massive beard
It followed me, it was bright all night
Then I gave it a little fright.

The tree got scared and ran away
Would I see it again?
Oh my, what a day!

Temi Smith (8)
The Firs School, Chester

The Dragon On The Moon

I saw a dragon wearing a wig,
The dragon was very big.
It looked at me when it gave me a cake,
I think it was fake.
I really wanted it to go away
But it just said, "No way!"
It flew higher and higher until it got to the moon,
Then it gave me a special balloon.
Suddenly, I realised the dragon was pleased
Because the dragon was on the moon,
Which is made out of cheese!

Lola May Bowden (8)
The Firs School, Chester

My Dad Is A Chicken!

My dad came home and wasn't the same
He'd forgotten mine and mummy's name
He started to cluck and grow a wing
Then I realised he was the king,
Just like that he was out of luck
Then he clucked "Seeds now!"
What a nightmare for the chick and cow
"Oh, how will I get my daddy back?
Please, Mummy, help me with a life hack!"

Josh Gratton (8)
The Firs School, Chester

The Weird Surfer On Rice

Once upon a time,
There was a surfer who surfed on rice,
Lots of people thought that he was pretty nice.
He surfed on brown rice, white rice
And sticky rice too.
He surfed on fried rice,
Boiled rice, old rice and new.
Nobody knew why he didn't surf on the sea,
Let's hope he doesn't surf on my rice pudding tea!

Tia Lily Hughes (9)
The Firs School, Chester

The Stupidly Dressed Dinosaur

There is a dinosaur who is very big
And everybody thinks he is wearing a wig.
The dinosaur is wearing a polka-dot shirt
And why is the dinosaur wearing a girl's skirt?
He likes to roam the empty streets
Wearing big boots too big for his feet.
I really don't know what to say,
I am just thankful he's gone away.

Jack O'Keefe (8)
The Firs School, Chester

I Can Eat Everything

I can eat a rainbow,
I can eat the sea,
I can eat a snowman,
I can eat a tree.

I love food so much,
My favourite time is tea.
My favourite drink is punch,
My least favourite drink is wee.

I can eat a monkey,
I can eat a bush,
I can eat a donkey,
I can eat slush.

William Edward Mallon (8)
The Firs School, Chester

My Teacher Is An Alien

My teacher is an alien
Oh, what has she done?
She looks like a potato
And smells like the burning sun
She makes me do silly maths
And has sloppy, green hair
When will I have my normal teacher back?
Because proper training
Is what my alien teacher lacks!

Abeer Vashisht (8)
The Firs School, Chester

Gummy Bears

Gummy bears have gummy arms,
Gummy feet and gummy legs
I like to hang my gummy bears
Out on gummy pegs!
One is red and one is blue,
One would always swim and one always flew.
My gummy bears are small and silly,
Bob, Jeff, Thomas and Billy.

Olly Jones (8)
The Firs School, Chester

My World Of Mother Nature!

Trees are everywhere, go green!
Animals have their shelter
Birds have the power of chirping
This is Mother Nature!

The clouds above the sky are blue
The sun is glistening a flash of light
Animals are leaving steps as a clue
Mountains look like an exquisite sight!

Flowers bloom on the grass
Rocks fall from the top
The weather has a different forecast
As rain comes but only a drop!

A sweet smell nourishes the air
And rivers in the countryside
Owls flap mid-air
"I love my planet!" Mother Nature replied!

Saanvi Nayak (10)
The Willows Primary School, Woodhouse Park

My Tea With The Mad Hatter

My tea with the Mad Hatter was interesting
You see, he really liked a jolly good natter
And took a slurp and a burp
Of his afternoon coffee
I sat facing his way
And he fed me for what seemed
Like the whole day
A tornado of biscuit crumbs
Rushed out of his mouth
And oh how he laughed!
He piled my plate high
Until it was practically touching the sky!
After our dinner, he handed me a bright red hat
And said, "Did you enjoy our dinner, Nat?"
So that was my tea with the Mad Hatter
And it was quite interesting, as you can see!

Mia McCaffery (10)
The Willows Primary School, Woodhouse Park

My Friend Leana

This is my friend Leana...

She is beautiful and caring
We fly all over the big, blue sky in loops and spins
Her wings are green and orange
And her fur is pale pink
When we see other people
Leana gives them a wink
Leana loves to eat crazy food
Called snozzleberries
And after lunch, we fly around
To watch everybody's tellies!
Leana is half bird and half tiger
But nothing like a spider
Her fur is soft and very silky
And at the end, it is curly
Leana is my best friend
And I wouldn't change her for the world.

Lucie Hannah Oxley (7)
The Willows Primary School, Woodhouse Park

Farting Monster

A popadom monster went to space
He wanted to see an alien face
He saw a cookie rocket and flew to the moon
He hoped he would be back very soon
He called in at Subway to get some snacks for the way
He set off to taste the chunky cheese
He got on the moon and his rocket broke at noon
Crash! The rocket broke down
Bosh! The monster farted all the way home.

Summer Kirkham (7)
The Willows Primary School, Woodhouse Park

Shrunk!

I woke up in the morning in an enormous bed
"What? I've shrunk!"
I walked on each step
I got downstairs
And climbed into a cupboard
And fell into the cereal box!
I nearly drowned in milk
I was about to be eaten!
I jumped out of the bowl,
I was free at last.
At the end of the day,
I grew to my size again.
"Wow, what a day!"

Hana Ahmed (9)
The Willows Primary School, Woodhouse Park

All Things Bright And Sweetiful

Flying lollipops, flying birds
Fairies eating mushrooms
And the best of all...
The trees are lollipops
And there are magnificent, talking cookies!
One of the fairies says, "Look, make a wish!
There's a flying cookie, quick!"
The baby fairy says, "Mummy, look!
My leaf tastes like a delicious, green apple!"

Dominique Palfreyman-Hawkes (8)
The Willows Primary School, Woodhouse Park

I Love Being A Unicorn

Pastel-pink covers my face
My blue mane swishes in the wind
My horn lets me bring up the sun at night
Follow the rainbow I must
Towards the sunlight
Oh how I love being a unicorn
I get admired every day
You should see the games I get to play!
Oh, how I love being a unicorn
Neigh, neigh, neigh!

Chelsea Roscoe (10)
The Willows Primary School, Woodhouse Park

The Wishing Plant

I've planted a seed in the middle of the fishes
Which happily grants many wishes
Underwater is the seed
Right next to the wriggly weed!
"Oh, I feel wet and cold!"
I should have been enough bold
All the splashes are on my face
This is a disgusting place
But what might this grow into?

Ikshita Singla (9)
The Willows Primary School, Woodhouse Park

Wonderland

I laugh, I shout,
Until I can't count.
The white queen's castle is where I will bow,
Falling down a rabbit hole is just wow!

For me to win is fifty-fifty
But I don't know
I'm here, it's the moment of my life
I have to defeat the dragon
Yes, I've done it!

Alexis Grace Daniels (9)
The Willows Primary School, Woodhouse Park

Zombie Apocalypse

Two evil zombies running down the street
Not the type of people you want to meet
One has one eye, the other has two toes
If you see them, you can't see their nose!
There are no people to scream or shout
I don't know what that's about
There are no humans to scream out!

Vincent Stringfellow (8)
The Willows Primary School, Woodhouse Park

The Tree And The Princess

The trees are dancing like ballerinas
The branches sway like butterflies
The leaves are falling like diamonds
The roots of the tree are wanting to skip and dance
The tree is like a princess wearing a brown dress with beautiful green hair
She has an invite to the wood summer ball.

Courtney Kavanagh (7)
The Willows Primary School, Woodhouse Park

Young Writers Information

We hope you have enjoyed reading this book – and that you will continue to in the coming years.

If you're a young writer who enjoys reading and creative writing, or the parent of an enthusiastic poet or story writer, do visit our website www.youngwriters.co.uk. Here you will find free competitions, workshops and games, as well as recommended reads, a poetry glossary and our blog. There's lots to keep budding writers motivated to write!

If you would like to order further copies of this book, or any of our other titles, then please give us a call or visit www.youngwriters.co.uk.

Young Writers
Remus House
Coltsfoot Drive
Peterborough
PE2 9BF
(01733) 890066
info@youngwriters.co.uk

Join in the conversation!
Tips, news, giveaways and much more!

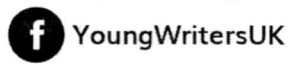

YoungWritersUK   @YoungWritersCW